Praise for Shannon Anderson and *Writing from Scratch*

"*Writing from Scratch* is one of the best resources I've come across for any educator looking to inspire young writers. Shannon Anderson provides practical instruction that helps students become not only better writers, but more joyful ones."

–**Trevor Muir**, Teacher, Author, Speaker

"During Shannon Anderson's 25-plus years of teaching, her expertise and creativity created enriching environments for student writers to thrive. Educators will find the lessons in *Writing from Scratch* appetizing and students will eat them up!"

–**Dr. Diana Bartnick Schmidt**, Professor Emerita of Education, Franklin College

"Unique and energizing, *Writing from Scratch* is a creative approach to a traditional topic–a must-have resource for educators that's guaranteed to grow young students into confident, engaged writers. Anderson's text is solid and provides elementary teachers with an easy-to-use treasury of explanations, strategies, scaffolding, and examples that are fun and effective."

–**Dr. Jeanneine P. Jones**, Professor Emeritus, University of North Carolina at Charlotte

WRITING FROM SCRATCH

WRITING FROM SCRATCH

LESSON PLANS TO BOOST YOUR CLASSROOM WRITING INSTRUCTION

Shannon Anderson

JB JOSSEY-BASS™

A Wiley Brand

Published by John Wiley & Sons, Inc., Hoboken, New Jersey.
Published simultaneously in Canada.

For general information on our other products and services, please contact our Customer Care Department within the United States at (800) 762-2974, outside the United States at (317) 572- 3993. For product technical support, you can find answers to frequently asked questions or reach us via live chat at https://support.wiley.com/s/.

If you believe you've found a mistake in this book, please bring it to our attention by emailing our reader support team at wileysupport@wiley.com with the subject line "Possible Book Errata Submission."

Wiley also publishes its books in a variety of electronic formats. Some content that appears in print may not be available in electronic formats. For more information about Wiley products, visit our web site at www.wiley.com.

Library of Congress Cataloging-in-Publication Data

Names: Anderson, Shannon, 1972- author.
Title: Writing from scratch : lesson plans to boost your classroom writing
  instruction / Shannon Anderson.
Description: [San Francisco, California] : Jossey-Bass, [2025] | Includes
  index.
Identifiers: LCCN 2024045071 (print) | LCCN 2024045072 (ebook) | ISBN
  9781394280995 (paperback) | ISBN 9781394281015 (adobe pdf) | ISBN
  9781394281008 (epub)
Subjects: LCSH: English language–Composition and exercises–Study and
  teaching (Elementary) | Lesson planning.
Classification: LCC LB1576 .A6195 2025 (print) | LCC LB1576 (ebook) | DDC
  372.62/3044–dc23/eng/20241014
LC record available at https://lccn.loc.gov/2024045071
LC ebook record available at https://lccn.loc.gov/2024045072

Cover Art & Design: Paul McCarthy

SKY10094340_122324

Contents

Author's Note

A cookbook for writing? Yes!

Of course, this isn't the kitchen variety. My goal is to provide you with easy-to-prepare recipes for your elementary classroom with heaping cups of confidence and a dash of fun.

What kind of "cookie baker" writing-lesson-maker are you? What I mean is, when teaching writing, much like baking cookies, there are different types of culinary comfort levels.

Baking Cookies	Teaching Writing
Prepackaged, Refrigerated Dough Just preheat the oven and bake the dough. Voilà! Not much room to make mistakes and no worries about not having all of the ingredients.	**Prerecorded, Video Lesson** Just pull up the video and show it. Voilà! No room for mistakes and the presenter demonstrates everything.
Cookie Box Mix Add a few of your own ingredients, as directed, but mostly follow the instructions given.	**Scripted Writing Program** Add a few of your own elements, as directed, but mostly follow the instructions given.
Pinterest Recipe Take some time to search for lessons with good ratings and pictured results. Use the recipe with your own students and resources.	**Pinterest or TPT Lesson** Take some time to search for lessons with good ratings and pictured results. Use the lesson with your own students and resources.
Made-from-Scratch Cookies Use your prior experience and knowledge of recipes and ingredients to create your own recipe. These are custom-made to fit the tastes and dietary needs of your personal cookie monsters who will be eating them.	**Made-from-Scratch Lesson** Use your prior experience and knowledge of lessons and resources to create your own lesson. These lessons are custom-made to fit the interests and needs of your personal classroom students who will be writing.

Do you feel comfortable with your "culinary" skills? I will admit that my confidence in the kitchen isn't at the Rachael Ray level. I'm more apt to use the refrigerated, premade dough or a box mix. In my training to be a "grown-up," I did not have cooking or baking lessons. And, since it wasn't a passion of mine, I never took the time to really learn.

Maybe you feel that way about writing. When I went through school as a student, the focus for writing lessons was more on the conventions. My teachers checked for correct grammar, punctuation, and capitalization more than for craft and creativity.

The other parameter to determine if we nailed a writing assignment was all about the length. Was it the required full page? A five-paragraph essay? A 10-page term paper?

I honestly do not recall receiving instruction on the craft of writing—how to use transitions, how to create a captivating hook, or techniques for adding a stronger voice.

In my research for this book, I looked at a study that scanned thousands of college course syllabi for education majors. There were all kinds of teaching methods classes for science, math, social studies, and literature. There were even methods of teaching art, music, and physical education classes for teachers. But, at the elementary teaching level, there were *very* few instances of designated methods of teaching a writing class. Is it any wonder why many elementary teachers do not feel equipped or confident about teaching writing in their elementary classrooms?

While this book is not going to replace a "Methods for Teaching Writing" class, I hope to give you some tools and ideas for growing your young writers. My philosophy for teaching writing is that we need to equip kids with specific skill-based lessons that can be applied in authentic writing experiences. **Our ultimate goal should not be just to develop the writing, but rather to develop our *students* as writers.** This goal was emphasized as a need in the NCTE (National Council of Teachers of English) "Position Statement on Writing Instruction in School," released in August 2022.

If we can deliver skill-based lessons in ways that are meaningful and fun, your writing block can be a time of day that both you and your students look forward to. When students see the purpose in the skills being taught and start to see it improving how they think as writers, they will be more engaged and start flexing their creative muscles.

This "cookbook" is formatted to offer a you-can-do-it approach. Just like a food cookbook, it isn't meant to be read front to back. You can search for a lesson that meets a current need or that you are just in the mood for.

You willl find a list of your ingredients (resources, materials, and mentor texts), appetizers (attention grabbers to whet your students' appetites for the lesson), a cooking demonstration (what you will model), directions (what the students will do), and dessert options (ideas for sharing or celebrating the work). I stir in some additional comments, notes, and best practice tips along the way.

This is not a stand-alone writing program, but rather a hearty supplement focused on boosting creativity and improving how your kids think about writing. These lessons will help you serve up lessons with confidence. Once you start to use these recipes, they may just inspire you to create some made-from-scratch recipes of your own!

Bon appétit!

Cooking Success Tips

- **Have kids write daily**. "As students write, they learn by doing. They try out different forms of writing, apply different strategies and approaches for producing text, and gain fluency with basic writing skills such as handwriting, spelling, and sentence construction." –International Literacy Association (2020), "Teaching Writing to Improve Reading Skills."

- **Learn, reflect, and brainstorm writing techniques with other teachers**. Sharing mentor text and prop ideas can multiply your resources. And "collective teacher efficacy" has an effect size of 1.39 on student achievement, according to John Hattie's Influences on Student Achievement in 2019.

- **Model writing in front of your students**. Share your thoughts out loud as you are working in front of them. Let them see your mistakes and aha moments. Professor Cassandra O'Sullivan Sachar, an associate English professor at Bloomsburg University, explains, "By showing our own missteps and then using strategies to improve what we've written, we teach valuable lessons about how the writing process works." This also allows students to understand expectations for an assignment and may inspire them with ideas to help them begin. It truly is a game changer when you model your lessons.

- **Provide authentic audiences and purposes for your students' writing.** According to Jennifer Jump, in *What the Science of Reading Says about Writing,* "decisions are driven by their [students'] awareness of task, audience, and purpose, which also informs their language choices and tone."

  Any type of writing can be more palatable when we provide opportunities for students to affect others with a message or story. It's important to remember that we can provide choices for them to share their stories and information too. They can use digital presentations, sound, images, or the written word. It's all communication and these are all using forms of writing. Providing authentic audiences for their work is a way to allow writers to see the impact of their words. It may be fun to write a fractured fairy tale, but to get kids to believe that writing is important, they have to have faith that their words and thoughts matter to someone.

- **Help kids see themselves as writers.** We need to be sure our students understand that they *are* writers. Sometimes they say, "I'm not a good writer," "I don't like writing," or "I don't know how to write." This fixed mindset can hamper their confidence and future success communicating with others. Students are all readers, but not because they read whole books and can talk about them. They are readers because they read the directions on a page, they understand the meaning in an illustration, and they read the lunch menu. Students don't avoid looking at a phone to read a text message because they don't like reading or claim not to be a reader.

We need to erase this mode of thinking that writing is only reports and essays about a given topic. Just like reading, writing is something we do all day long. We write to-do lists, we sketch pictures to help us remember things, we write notes and texts. Yes, we also write stories, poems, and reports, but that isn't the only kind of writing and that isn't what defines us as writers.

Once kids understand that we are all readers and writers, we can help them realize that maybe they just need to grow in a certain type of writing. Maybe a topic was assigned that they didn't know much about or enjoy. This shouldn't ruin a particular genre forever, and it shouldn't cause them to feel like they can't write because the words weren't coming to them easily or joyfully on a few occasions.

Just as most people are not good at *all* sports, that doesn't mean that we are not good at *any* sports. You may be a great basketball player but have a lot of room to improve when playing tennis. That being said, there are some people who are not inclined toward any sports and there will be some people who are not inclined to enjoy most kinds of writing. Keep the focus on the fact that there are many kinds of writing and that some types may not come as naturally as others.

- **Become a writer.** This may sound extreme, but you'll notice a difference in how you approach writing in your classroom if *you* are a writer, and not just someone who sends a text message or is a writer during writing block at school. Really be a writer. It will change the way you teach it and the way you feel about it.

When you start to do this, you'll find yourself sharing things with the kids about your discoveries. It could be about your process, your word choices, your struggles, or how you finally finished something. *This matters.* The kids will see you as a real writer for real reasons and they will start to write for real too.

You can start with a small step. Get a writer's notebook or journal. *Record* thoughts in it each day. Reflect on what you're grateful for, jot down teaching ideas, or take notes in it when you watch a webinar. If you write a sticky note about something you want to do for a lesson, put that note in your notebook. If you write an idea on a napkin at a restaurant, stick it in your notebook when you get home. Show this notebook to your students. Let them see the messy, fun ways we collect ideas. Let them know that ideas are important. They are scraps of knowledge that can be used as compost for our stories!

How to Use This Book

Like most recipe books, this one assumes a certain level of competency in order to use the lessons. For example, you wouldn't use a cookbook to learn how to work your stove, measure ingredients, or sift flour. **This is not a "How to Write" book. It's more of a "How to Grow Your Writers" book.** It is best suited for students who are already able to write sentences. (I could write an entire book on how to get kids from writing a string of letters to writing sentences, but this is not that book.)

As an elementary teacher, I planned based on an overall view of what I needed to cover for the year, but fine-tuned what to teach each day based on needs. There was *never* a lack of needs. With endless possibilities to include in this book, I tried to choose lesson ideas and exercises for improving writing techniques that may happen in different stages of your writers' development. I've organized the lessons into writing goals. They are not in a particular order, though some of the "Generating Ideas" lessons are great for starting a new school year.

Preheating the Oven

At the beginning of the year, it's recommended to set your table with some items and procedures that will prepare students for success during writing time.

Author Chair

You'd be surprised how easy it is to score an inexpensive chair to use for your author chair.

1. Go to garage sales, consignment shops, flea markets, or online sale sites, or ask friends and family for a wooden stool, bench, or chair.
2. Sand it down. Buy craft paints in various colors and some paintbrushes.
3. Spread out garbage bags or plastic under the chair in your classroom.
4. Put students in groups of three or four to take turns painting parts of the chair.
5. Allow the chair to dry overnight.
6. Once dry, write "Author's Chair" somewhere. Then allow students to put their names on the chair with a permanent marker all over the chair surface.
7. Voilà, you have an author chair! A place of honor to sit that shows anyone who comes into your room that writing is valued there.
8. During writing block, allow kids to share their writing from the author chair. Other students gather on the floor around the author chair to listen.
9. When someone is doing an amazing job on their writing, making great progress, using a creative spin, sharing a writing they did at home for fun, or any other thing worth celebrating, allow them to put their name in a drawing.
10. At the end of the year, draw out a name. That child gets to take the chair home to keep. Start all over the next summer with a different chair.

NOTE You can use other types of chairs besides wooden ones, of course. For example, you could get a director's-style chair and have kids sign their names on the canvas seat and back.

Writers' Notebooks

Having a writer's notebook can build anticipation for the writing that will happen in your room. It is a place where students can brainstorm, have sections for favorite words and phrases, take notes for various lessons, or practice techniques.

Kick off the year by bringing in a writing notebook of your own. Show the kids what you have in yours. If you don't have one, you can create one as a model or find examples online to show kids how authors use them.

On the day that you have kids painting the author chair, the other kids could be taking time to decorate their writing notebooks. You can provide magazines to cut pictures and words from, stickers, and other embellishments. Let them create a notebook that inspires them.

Writing Folders

Throughout this book, you will find lessons focused on specific skills. These are meant to continue to be built upon. When a student has practiced a skill, have them keep that page in their folder. There will be times they refer back to lessons in the folder. There will also be times that a lesson will be built upon and students can add onto a work in progress.

At times, you may have anchor papers, reference sheets, or tools that can be kept in their folders. For example, in the Generating Ideas section, students will have a ME Page and an Expert List to keep in their folders.

Procedures

Ideally, you want to make time for writing opportunities every day. One way to reduce wasted time is to create procedures. What have you noticed takes time away from the instruction and practice during your writing time? How will you handle access to writing folders and notebooks? Will kids have paper at their space or need to get some? How will you handle questions and spelling during practice time?

All of these items need to be considered and taught to allow for maximum productivity and minimal distraction. You'd be surprised how many minutes you gain daily by teaching procedures for all of the transition times, supply procurement, and expectations.

Spelling

I noticed students often got hung up on spelling their words correctly during writing. Although I never put an emphasis on having to spell everything correctly, some kids aren't happy with just "sounding out" a word. They want to know how to spell it. I found ways to help them spell words, with minimal fuss. For the lower grades, I created a "My Try" page. This saved lots of time and stress.

My Try	Correct Spelling

Students could get this out from their writing folders when they want help spelling a word. They simply try to spell it in the left column and when I see this, I come by and write in the correct spelling across from it. It's quick and painless.

For the older elementary grades, I allowed my students to look up spellings on their devices. (This is what real writers do, after all.)

Making the Most of Your Time

You have a lot of control over the transitions between hooking your students, modeling the focus skill, and releasing kids to practice because you are the one leading. When it comes to the time between practicing and sharing, though, if kids are engaged, it can be hard to get them to stop writing. (Really, I promise!)

I teach a procedure that seamlessly gets kids to stop writing and head back to the author chair for sharing time.

1. During the practice time, I am scouting out good examples of the skill we are practicing. I let a few students know that I'd like them to bring their work with them when we share that day.

2. Use a signal of your choosing for kids to stop writing. This signal means they need to put down their pencils and head back to the author chair.

3. The students who have been chosen for sharing are lined up by the author chair.

The way I practice this procedure is by letting kids know my signal. It can be a bell sound, a phrase, or a clapping sequence. Use whatever works for you. I simply say, "Okay, pencils down." To practice, I have kids start writing their first, middle, and last name. After a few seconds, I say, "Okay, pencils down." No matter how far they've gotten, they must stop writing and put down their pencils and head back to the author chair. I do this again by having them start writing the alphabet. Again, I say, "Okay, pencils down," and they stop on whatever letter they were on.

These may seem silly, but it gets them to understand and remember the signal. They get that it doesn't mean to stop writing after your last thought or sentence. It means stop writing on the letter in the middle of the word they are on. You'll be amazed at how quickly they are ready to share.

Purposeful Planning

Some teachers have writing programs that their schools use. If this is the case, you could use some of these ideas and lessons as a supplement to lessons you already teach. You may particularly find the creative writing exercises or poetry lessons engaging. Other teachers do not have a specific writing curriculum and may be creating their own lessons for writing. For my first 23 years of teaching, I had no program or curriculum to use and I actually loved that! I enjoyed coming up with authentic writing experiences and I based my lessons on needs I noticed throughout the year. I saved my lessons to use again and again, tweaking and improving them each year.

Many schools use writing prompts at certain times of the year as benchmark writing assessments for each grade level. The entire grade level uses the same prompt and you are able to discuss how students are doing as a grade level. Depending on your state standards, you will have different genres to focus on for these prompts. When I taught third grade, for example, our standards required us to teach personal narratives, opinion writing, and informational writing. We would set dates for when each one needed to be completed. As a grade level, we would get together to discuss how our students did on their prompts and share lesson ideas to help each other in areas of noted need.

I should note that I don't recommend taking your three to four prompts and teaching only those genres. I've seen some schools do a different genre per quarter. They may do letter-writing for a whole nine-week period! Of course, you want to focus on the specific ingredients needed for a genre you are getting ready to assess. If you are teaching personal narratives, you would want to teach kids how to write a beginning and ending for that type of writing. You would want to teach them how to narrow the focus of their topic and provide interesting details. You wouldn't want them only writing personal narratives for a quarter of the year, though. Be sure to vary the skills and genres you cover throughout the year.

Recipe: Apples to Apples

Notes from the Chef

One way that you can gain even more information from prompts is to use the same prompts for all of your elementary grade levels. Year after year, kindergarten, first grade, second grade, third grade, fourth grade, and fifth grade all would do the same prompt. After assessing these with students, you can save them in a writing folder that gets passed to the next year's teacher.

Besides being able to compare apples to apples each year, seeing each student's writing progress on the same prompt, students get to see their own progress as well. I love that before the school year even started, I had a peek at the writing strengths and needs of my students. It was like having a pre-assessment that they already completed in my hands.

Ingredients

Last year's writing for each student
Resources for the genre you are working on (mentor texts, video clips, articles, etc.)
Writing prompt

Appetizer

Share the prompt you will be working on. For example, maybe you're working on opinion writing and the prompt is "Which is a better pet, a cat or a dog?" This should be the same prompt that your students had last year in the previous grade. Pass out their papers from the year before. If you are teaching third or fourth grade, students will have several examples to see. They normally marvel over how far they have come since kindergarten, when they were just drawing the animal and using a few words!

The point of this exercise is for students and teachers to see the growth of individual students on the same prompts. Sometimes it's harder to see growth when we're using different prompts each year. The writing of the student could be affected by a lack of background knowledge or experience. In this case, we don't know if they're struggling to write or struggling because they just don't know enough about the topic.

Cooking Demonstration and Practice

1. On the first day, the students will just be gathering information about the prompt, planning, and taking notes. You can provide books, articles, and show video clips. When I was working on the dog/cat opinion writing, I was sharing information about things we know about cats and dogs. I had pet care books and articles, videos about dogs and cats, resources from veterinary websites, and we all shared from personal experience, too.

2. During this phase, students are deciding which animal they think makes a better pet. They can choose the same animal they picked last year, or change their mind and pick the other one. The point is that they are writing to the same prompt.

3. On the next day, allow students to write their piece. They can use all of their notes and they are welcome to use the resources in the room. This is what real writers do when they're writing.

4. On the third day, allow students to use an editing checklist. (See "Check, Please!" in Chapter 18.) After checking off everything on the list, they can move on to self-assessing their piece using whatever rubric you use for this genre.

5. Collect the writing and self-assessment rubrics.

Dessert

Since these are formal prompts for assessment, use the "Teacher and Student Conferences" lesson (Chapter 20) to meet with each student and grade their work in front of them. After students set new goals for themselves, you can copy their work and rubric for them to keep and then also keep a copy in the folder that will be passed on to next year's teacher.

Main Ingredients for Writing

Writers need to be aware of six essential ingredients:

- Generating Ideas
- Word Choices
- Organization
- Making It Flow
- Emotion
- Grammar

Just as a good recipe has key ingredients to create a delightful flavor, the components for good writing must all work together to create a delightful read. The fun part is being creative with the amount of each ingredient and playing around with how we alter ingredients to make new and interesting recipes.

Whether we call them components, traits, or elements, these are basic ingredients that we make writerly decisions about as we compose and revise. We may do writing exercises that teach these in isolation but students need to ultimately understand that real writers use all of these pieces together, in concert.

Each of these ingredients can look different in each genre. For example, the way you would organize a persuasive piece of writing is much different than how you would organize a personal narrative or letter. There are many ways you can introduce these ingredients to your students at the beginning of the year.

Recipes for Reviewing

This lesson is intended to whet your students' appetite for writing, while using this culinary theme. The props provide visuals to aid in remembering the various ingredients for healthy writing habits. Your students may even come up with some clever cooking analogies of their own as the year progresses!

Recipe: Writing

Ingredients

Baking supplies, such as:

Mixing bowl
Whisk
Spice containers
Measuring cups
Apron
Heart-shaped plate
Mixing spoon or spatula
Recipe template pages

Recipe for

INGREDIENTS:

_____   _____
_____   _____
_____   _____

STEPS:

_____
_____
_____
_____
_____
_____
_____
_____
_____
_____
_____
_____
_____

Appetizer

1. Put on your apron and set up the baking supplies listed above. I labeled my items with the use of a Cricut® machine. (You can use a label maker, or just use sticky notes if you don't want to have permanently designated kitchen supplies for your classroom writing lessons.)

   Here are examples of my labels:

   > Bowl: **Writing from Scratch**
   >
   > Whisk: **Creative Whisk**
   >
   > Spice Containers: **Hyperbole, Idiom, Synonym, Simile, Onomatopoeia, Alliteration** (and other figurative language devices, depending on your grade level)
   >
   > Funnel: **Stay Focused**
   >
   > Spoon: **Mix It Up!**
   >
   > Measuring Cups: **Ideas, Word Choice, Making It Flow, Organization, Emotion, Grammar**
   >
   > Tongs: **Pick the Best**
   >
   > Heart-shaped plate: **Write From Your Heart**
   >
   > Ketchup and mustard squirters: **Emotions, Senses**
   >
   > Plastic Hamburger or Sandwich: **Intro** (top bun); **Body** (meat); **Conclusion** (bottom bun); **Details, Examples, Trials** (other toppings, like lettuce, tomato, and pickles, depending on the type of genre)
   >
   > Dollhouse-sized oven: **Make It and Bake It**

2. Discuss how cooking or baking something delicious can be a lot like writing a story that is delightful. How are they the same and different? What would be a recipe for a good piece of writing?

3. Hold up each labeled item and go further with the analogy.

Cooking Demonstration and Practice

1. Use the measuring cups to discuss the main ingredients for good writing, one at a time. Pass out the recipe template page for students to take notes on. Example discussion could include:

   Generating Ideas: This ingredient helps us to figure out what to write about and how to focus. The tongs can represent picking the best ideas from those you have gathered. Real writers do a lot of brainstorming and make lots of lists, in order to have options. The first idea that comes to mind is not always the best one. It is important to think about all different kinds of ideas as you write.

The funnel is another idea-related prop. It is important to focus in on your idea, or topic. You need to be able to narrow down topics to make them more interesting and focused.

Word Choice: This ingredient helps us find creative and interesting ways to share our information or stories. You can use the spice containers with the figurative language device labels to show ways we can make our word choices more interesting and playful. For example, instead of saying that someone doesn't understand, you could use a simile: "He was as confused as a chameleon in a bucket of crayons!"

Making It Flow: This ingredient helps us to make our language flow in ways that use variety and word patterns. You can use your spoon or spatula to explain how we need to mix up our sentence lengths and structures to add variety. We don't want a lot of short and choppy sentences together. And we don't want to start all of our sentences with the same stem over and over.

Organization: This ingredient gives our writing a logical structure or order. Show the hamburger and its parts. For younger grades, you may have each part of the hamburger just as sentences to form one paragraph. For older kids, each part could represent a paragraph in a longer story or nonfiction piece.

Emotion: This ingredient helps the reader feel something expressed by the author. Your ketchup or mustard container labeled "Emotions" can be used to talk about showing how characters feel through dialogue, point of view, voice, and other techniques. The other condiment, labeled "Senses," is about adding sensory details so that the reader can feel more like they are a part of the story. They can picture the scenes in their mind.

Grammar: This ingredient ensures that the spelling and mechanics of the piece are correct to help with readability and presentation. An analogy that works for this is the oven. We can add all of the right ingredients and mix them well, but if we don't bake it at the right temperature or the right length of time, we aren't going to be able to eat it. It may be too undercooked or burnt. It's the same with our writing. We can have the best ideas and organize them well, but if our spelling and punctuation make it too difficult to be read and understood, no one can enjoy our writing. You can share this quote from culinary legend Barbara Kafka: "Baking is about transformation. Turning flour into cakes, eggs into custard, and ideas into something real."

2. Put students in pairs to come up with the recipe for a good piece of writing, keeping the main ingredients in mind. Here is an example.

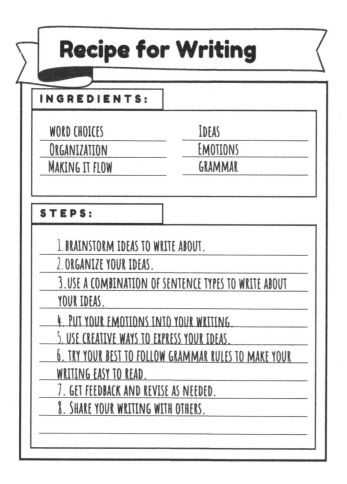

Recipe for Writing

INGREDIENTS:

WORD CHOICES   IDEAS
ORGANIZATION   EMOTIONS
MAKING IT FLOW   GRAMMAR

STEPS:

1. BRAINSTORM IDEAS TO WRITE ABOUT.
2. ORGANIZE YOUR IDEAS.
3. USE A COMBINATION OF SENTENCE TYPES TO WRITE ABOUT YOUR IDEAS.
4. PUT YOUR EMOTIONS INTO YOUR WRITING.
5. USE CREATIVE WAYS TO EXPRESS YOUR IDEAS.
6. TRY YOUR BEST TO FOLLOW GRAMMAR RULES TO MAKE YOUR WRITING EASY TO READ.
7. GET FEEDBACK AND REVISE AS NEEDED.
8. SHARE YOUR WRITING WITH OTHERS.

Dessert

Allow a few groups to share their recipes or compile them into a Writing Recipe Book for the classroom.

Recipe: Songs

Notes from the Chef

This is a favorite activity to review the various ingredients. As you know, songs help us remember things and also make the learning more fun. You'll need to think of several songs with tunes that kids will know. After taking notes, your notes will be composed into songs to go with those tunes.

Ingredients List

Chart paper
Markers
Device to video record the songs (such as a phone)

Appetizer

Ask students why it's important to have writing skills. Take notes on chart paper or your whiteboard. Items may include things like:

- To make a grocery list
- To write a thank-you card
- To create a story to enjoy
- To record history
- To email someone important information
- To take notes to learn and remember things

Then give a tune to a well-known song, such as "Twinkle, Twinkle, Little Star" or "The Hokey Pokey." Together, compose a song with your notes about writing to the tune you choose. Sing the song together afterward.

Maybe it becomes something like this, to the tune of "Row, Row, Row Your Boat":

We write grocery lists,
And we story tell.
We can write a thank-you card,
Or wish somebody well.

We can take some notes.
We can write a song.
We can record memories,
We write all day long.

Cooking Demonstration and Practice

You can vary this lesson based on the age of your students and if you want to try to collaborate with other classrooms. There are six basic ingredients for good writing, so decide if you want to put kids into groups within your classroom, pair them with a partner, have different classrooms in your grade level take on one or two ingredients, or some other variation. Here is one way you could do this.

1. As a class, review and take notes on anchor charts for each of the ingredients during your writing block. Examples for notes could include:

   a. **Generating Ideas**: Focused topic, relevant details, and background knowledge and research

   b. **Word Choices**: Strong verbs, specific nouns, creative word play, description, and sensory details

   c. **Organization**: Beginning, middle, and ending planned, transitions, and logical sequence of events

   d. **Making It Flow**: Complete thoughts and sentences, variety of sentence beginnings and lengths, and smooth readability

   e. **Emotion**: Audience awareness, attitude and feelings show, and authentic

   f. **Grammar**: Capitalization, punctuation, subject and verb agreement, and spelling

      Each day, review and take notes on a different ingredient until you have covered all six.

2. Put kids in your class into groups of four or five students. Give each group one of the anchor charts with the notes for their ingredient. Give each group a song to use for their tune.

3. The groups will come up with song lyrics to go with their ingredient.

4. Create a brief introduction for students to share about the trait.

Dessert

For each trait, have students share their introductory information about the trait. Then have each group sing their song. In this way, all of the ingredients will be reviewed for kids to remember. You can video the introductions and songs and stream them together as one video to share at different points in the year for review or for fun.

Generating Ideas

Why is it necessary to frontload with brainstorming and preplanning? This not only saves time but also helps lessen the number of demands on the **executive functions** required for writing. According to *The Writing Revolution: A Guide to Advancing Thinking Through Writing in All Subjects and Grades* by Judith C. Hochman and Natalie Wexler (Wiley, 2017), executive functions are "cognitive processes, housed primarily in the prefrontal cortex of the brain, that enable us to perform a series of actions and that are essential to good writing."

I'm sure you've witnessed that moment when you turn the lesson over for the kids to practice a skill you've just demonstrated and they stare at the blank page or screen, unable to begin. This is because they are trying to process the skill they are supposed to try and they also have to figure out what content to use to apply the skill. If we can remove the content part and have that planned out ahead of time, they can get to work on using the skill right away.

The lessons in this section are meant for generating topics and ideas to write about throughout the year *and* for brainstorming within a topic.

A Picture Is Worth a Thousand Words

Isn't this true? When kids see a picture of something from their lives, they want to share everything about it. Whether it's a picture where they are dressed in a funny costume, are at a special place, or of a favorite pet, pictures bring back all of the memories and stories associated with them.

At a parent night or in a letter, request that parents send in 10-12 pictures that may evoke some memories and story ideas. (If parents want the pictures back, you could make color copies of them and send the photos back.) These pictures can be stored in the students' writing folders. Or, if your school has one-to-one tablets, you could ask your students to take some pictures of special people, places, and things to store on their camera roll on their device. At various times during your writing block, you can have students choose a picture to use for various writing lessons. This will save lots of time, since kids won't have to think about what to write about. It will also create opportunities to write about things they know and care about, which will make writing about it so much more enjoyable and engaging.

Recipe: ME Page

Notes from the Chef

We never seem to have enough time to devote to writing. When it comes to practicing a skill that you've worked on for that day's lesson, you don't want kids to be stumped on what topic to write about to apply it. Many times kids may just stare at the empty page or blank screen, frozen, unable to think of what to write about. These activities will frontload lots of ideas at the beginning of the year. Problem solved!

Ingredients

- ME Page PDF
- Prompts

Appetizer: Surprise! You're Writing a Story!

1. Review what a noun is. Define proper nouns.

2. Say, "Surprise! You're going to write a story that uses a variety of proper nouns. You have 10 minutes to write your story about anything. Go!"

3. Start a timer.

4. Stop the timer after five minutes and discuss how hard it was to figure out what to write about when you have no preparation. There may even be some students who didn't start at all because they couldn't come up with a topic.

5. Discuss how much more they might have written if there was a plan in place for what they could write about first. The focus could then be on the skill (using proper nouns) instead of on the content of the story.

Cooking Demonstration and Practice

1. Pass out the ME PDF and use one on your document camera to project. (If you do not have a document camera, you can draw a giant ME on your whiteboard in bubble letters. Be sure to take a picture of it if you do it this way, for future use.)

2. Explain your purpose for the lesson: to provide lots of ideas for future use in writing practice time. Kids will fill their ME Page with things from their lives that they may want to write about for future lessons.

3. As you prompt kids with ideas to add to their page, you will do the same on your ME Page, to model what you're asking them to do. Prompts could include:

   - Who lives in your home? List your family members.
   - Do you have any pets? List them (past and present, if desired).
   - Have you gone on a vacation or to a cool place? Where?
   - Have you ever broken a bone or had to get stitches?
   - Have you ever won an award for something?
   - Did you ever have to move to a different home?
   - What is a time someone really surprised you?
   - Have you ever met someone famous?
   - What is the best gift you've ever received?

4. Choose one item from your own ME Page and write about it using some proper nouns in your sentences. Do this on the document camera or whiteboard and model your thinking as you write.

5. Have students choose one item from their list. Tell them they have 10 minutes to write about that one thing, using some proper nouns in their sentences.

Dessert

1. As you go around to assist, spot great examples.

2. Choose one to two students to share their story.

3. Have students go back to the author chair (sharing area).

4. Allow your chosen students to take a turn sharing.

5. Have students save their ME Page in their writing folders.

Recipe: Expert List

Notes from the Chef

This is similar to the ME Page concept, but concentrating on things that kids know a lot about. This list will come in handy for all kinds of writing throughout the year, especially nonfiction genres where they may need to share some expertise.

Ingredients

EXPERT LIST

- Expert List PDF
- Prompts

Appetizer: Expert Extraordinaire

1. Think of something you are good at and bring props or items to share. If you're a scrapbooker, for instance, you could bring in your tools, stickers, and paper.

2. Share a little bit about what you know about your skill.

3. Ask if they would agree that you may know more about it than someone else in the class or school.

4. Explain that you are an Expert Extraordinaire at that particular thing, compared to others with little or no experience.

Cooking Demonstration and Practice

1. Pass out the Expert List PDF and use one on your document camera to project. (If you do not have a document camera, you can write on your whiteboard.)

2. Explain your purpose for the lesson: to provide more ideas for future use in writing practice time. Kids will fill their Expert List with things they may know a lot about.

3. As you prompt kids with ideas to add to their page, you will do the same on your Expert List, to model what you're asking them to do. Prompts could include:

   - Do you play any sports?
   - What clubs do you enjoy?
   - Do you play an instrument?
   - Do you like to draw, act, dance, or sing?
   - Do you help in a garden?
   - Do you take care of pets or other animals?
   - Do you know about your parents' jobs?
   - Are you good at a certain game?
   - What are you good at making (food, crafts, inventions, etc.)?

Dessert

1. Have kids choose one item from their Expert List.

2. Allow kids to get into partners. Have them orally share all they know about the item from their list with their partner.

3. Have students save their Expert List in their writing folder for future use.

Generating Focused Topics

Focusing in on a topic makes the writing more interesting and provides students with the opportunity to research more detailed information.

We could write an article about the county fair, but that is a huge idea. We could say a little bit about the different animals, something about the rides, a mention of the games, how the queen contest works, or what it's like to stay all week at the fair. But to get readers interested, we need to focus in on the one part we can bring to life. We need to become an expert on that one aspect and share as much detail about the focus as possible. Otherwise, our writing just becomes a big list, and everyone's story would be about the same.

Think about having the topic of the ocean. That's pretty big! How could you narrow that down? Now narrow it again. How about again? When you really get focused, you create something that will be more meaningful. Here is an example:

Ocean > Ocean Animals > Sharks > Great White Sharks > How Great Sharks Hunt

Recipe: Zooming In on Ideas

Notes from the Chef

This lesson will help kids see how to take something big and zoom down into one smaller idea. This will help kids to go deeper about their topic, rather than wider.

Ingredients

Zoom, by Istvan Banyai
ME Page

Appetizer

Show the book *Zoom* by Istvan Banyai, a wordless picture book where each page shows images being zoomed in on. Or use this video of the book being shown: `https://youtu.be/Kgi-RCEjOLw?si=tCqgIcHesqaGodFk`. Discuss the animals and people featured in the book.

Cooking Demonstration and Practice

1. There are many people and animals in the book *Zoom*. If you were to write about them, the story would be very long and you probably wouldn't have a lot of details about each one.

2. Sample script: "Think about the people and animals in your life. You could write about all of them, but you probably wouldn't go into a lot of detail because there are so many. My guess is our stories would be pretty similar, listing family members and pets. Today, I'm going to pick *one* family member or pet from my ME Page and write about them."

3. Choose a person or animal from your ME Page. Hold up a finger for each detail you can think of about the person or animal and share. Say, "If you can't think of at least five details, choose a different one." Model by writing lots of details about why the person or animal is important to you, what they look like, and what their personality is like on a doc cam, anchor chart, or whiteboard.

4. Have students choose a person or animal from their ME Page.

5. Have students list things they know orally first, counting details on their fingers.

6. Have students write about the person or animal in detail, like you did.

Dessert

During sharing time, have several students share their descriptions.

Recipe: Narrowing Your Focus

Notes from the Chef

This is another chance for kids to learn to focus in, using a visual gimmick to help them. Using a "zoomer," or toilet paper tube, will provide a memorable device to help them think about narrowing their focus when writing.

Ingredients

Toilet paper or paper towel cardboard tubes ("zoomers")

Appetizer

Have students look out the window in your classroom or hallway. Have them share the various things they see outside by turning and talking to someone about what they observe. Are their examples similar? Would it be very exciting to write about everything you see outside and then hear everyone share their descriptions about the same things?

Cooking Demonstration and Practice

1. Take a toilet paper or paper towel cardboard tube, a "zoomer," and walk over to the window. Look through the tube at *one* object.

2. Tell the kids about the object you focused in on. Model by writing about that object with details such as what it is, what function it serves, what it looks like, why you focused on it, and so on.

3. Pass out cardboard tubes to your students. Allow them to come to the window and focus on one object outside this time.

4. Have students write a description about their object, similar to what you demonstrated.

Dessert

Allow several students to share their descriptions during sharing time.

Adding Ideas: Elaboration Techniques

We need to help students learn to narrow their focus for topics. But we also need to teach them how to expand on details once it is focused in. Sometimes students aren't sure how to add to a story, a persuasive piece, or a nonfiction topic.

There are techniques for putting more information into a piece of fiction writing, such as adding dialogue or sensory details. When we are persuading someone, we need to have plenty of reasons, facts, and examples. In all writing, we can do a lot with our word choices to add some flavor. (We will get into that more in Chapter 13, "Word Choice.") Here are example recipes for elaborating on stories and persuasive writings.

Recipe: Adding Details and Dialogue

Notes from the Chef

Sometimes kids just don't have enough meat to their stories, but they aren't really sure how to beef them up. One suggestion is to add some details and dialogue. This not only gives their story more quantity, but it also improves the quality because the reader gets more information to help them experience what is happening.

Ingredients

Boring written scene examples
Mixing bowl
Measuring cups

Appetizer

Prepare a short, boring written scene/part of a story. For example:

Mary Jane had a birthday coming up. Her mom always surprised her with something on the morning of her birthday.
    When she woke up the next day, she waited and waited for her surprise.
After lunch, her dad showed up with a box with a puppy inside!

Place the piece of writing in a mixing bowl and ask students what they could add to give it more excitement and flavor. You could have measuring cups labeled "Details" and "Dialogue."

Cooking Demonstration and Practice

1. With the first measuring cup, "Details," think aloud as you add more details.

   Mary Jane had a birthday coming up. Her mom always surprised her with something on the morning of her birthday. **DETAIL: One year, her mom had a singing quartet outside her bedroom door!**

   When she woke up the next day, she waited and waited for her surprise. After lunch, her dad showed up with a box. **DETAIL: The box was big and seemed heavy for him to carry. She tore open the lid.** There was a puppy inside!

2. With the second measuring cup, "Dialogue," think aloud as you add some dialogue. This could include internal dialogue (thoughts) or spoken dialogue.

   Mary Jane had a birthday coming up. Her mom always surprised her with something on the morning of her birthday. One year, her mom had a singing quartet outside her bedroom door!

   When she woke up the next day, she waited and waited for her surprise. **INTERNAL DIALOGUE:** *Did Mom forget about my birthday this year?* After lunch, her dad showed up with a box. The box was big and seemed heavy for him to carry.

   > **DIALOGUE: "We know you're excited to see your surprise," said Mom. "And your surprise is excited to see you too!" said Dad.**
   > She tore open the lid. There was a puppy inside!

3. Prepare another short, boring written scene/part of a story. You can send this digitally so they can edit/add details on their devices, project it on a whiteboard, or pass it out on paper. Challenge students to add at least one detail, one internal dialogue, and one spoken dialogue.

Dessert

Allow several students to share their new versions of the scene.

Recipe: Adding Oomph to Persuade

Notes from the Chef

This one can be a lot of fun and has the potential for some humor! With the chance at an authentic audience and possible change in a policy, circumstance, or reward, kids can't wait to contribute ideas.

Ingredients

I LOVE Strawberries! by Shannon Anderson

Appetizer

Read "I LOVE Strawberries!" How does Jolie convince her parents that she is old enough and responsible enough to grow her own strawberry patch? How could you convince someone to let you do something? You can add some "oomph" to your plea by adding reasons and facts.

Think of a real example of something you're willing to let the kids do so that they have an authentic reason and motivation for writing persuasively.
Ideas could be:

- Growing some kind of fruit or vegetable in the classroom hydroponically or in a school garden. What should we grow and why?
- Getting a class pet. What should we get and why?
- Working with the school lunch administrator to get to plan one of the meals. What should they cook? Why would it be a good idea?
- Convincing the guidance counselor to get a therapy dog for the school. How could you help fund it? Why would the dog benefit the school?
- Installing a Little Free Library outside the school. How would it help? Why is it a good idea?
- Getting a Buddy Bench for the playground. How could it be funded? Why is it needed?

Pick a different idea as an example to model, maybe something you want to convince the principal to do, like getting to wear jeans every Friday. Write your opinion statement.

Teachers should be allowed to wear jeans every Friday.

Think aloud as you add some "oomph" to your persuasive essay. Add facts, reasons, and/or examples.

Teachers should be allowed to wear jeans every Friday.

> **REASON:** Having a wardrobe of fancy clothes is expensive.
> **FACT:** Teachers don't make a lot of money.
> **REASON:** People are more comfortable when they can be more casual.
> **FACT:** Elementary teachers are on the floor, kneel next to student desks, and move around a lot. Stretchy, casual clothes are better suited for this.
> **REASON:** Teachers can relate to their students better when they are dressed like them.
> **EXAMPLE:** Being able to wear a class or school spirit shirt (with jeans) can unite the class. Just like a sports team, bonding with what makes us alike can be powerful.
> **REPEAT REASONS:** Teachers getting to wear jeans can help with a teacher's budget, help them feel more comfortable, and bond them with their students. If they can't wear them every day, then just on Fridays would be a first step.

Teachers should be allowed to wear jeans every Friday.

Having a wardrobe of fancy clothes is expensive. Teachers don't make a lot of money.

People are more comfortable when they can be more casual. Elementary teachers are on the floor, kneel next to student desks, and move around a lot. Stretchy, casual clothes are better suited for this.

Teachers can relate to their students better when they are dressed like them. Being able to wear a class or school spirit shirt (with jeans) can unite the class. Just like a sports team, bonding with what makes us alike can be powerful.

Teachers getting to wear jeans can help with a teacher's budget, help them feel more comfortable, and bond them with their students. If they can't wear them every day, then just on Fridays would be a first step.

(Keep in mind that you would save this writing for a later lesson when working on transitions. Today's focus is adding "oomph" when you are trying to persuade.)

Cooking Demonstration and Practice

1. Share whichever scenario you're willing to carry out with your students. Have the kids decide what they want to convince their audience to do. If you're deciding on a class pet or to grow a particular kind of food, have each student write their own statements. For example: I think we should grow cucumbers in the classroom.

2. Have students come up with three reasons and three facts and/or examples to back them up.

3. Have students conclude by restating the three reasons they think the audience should be convinced to do what they are stating.

Dessert

Have students share their persuasive mini-essays with the class. Take a vote on whatever action they think should happen if it is convincing fellow students (class pet, plant, etc.). If it is changing the lunch menu or something that would need a different audience, consider inviting the decision-makers into your room to hear them read their requests.

Organization

When we are preparing a cheesecake, there is an organized way to make it. You can't just throw all of the graham cracker crumbs, butter, sugar, cream cheese, fruit, and vanilla in one bowl and mix it up. You have to put together the ingredients for the graham cracker crust first and bake it. Then you can mix the cheesecake filling. Finally, you can top it with cherries or strawberries, or whatever you like.

Just like the cheesecake, we have to help kids understand that stories, letters, persuasive essays, articles, poems, and other genres all have an order to them. We can't just randomly spray the page with our thoughts and scatter details wherever we feel like it. There are different ways to organize the different types of writing.

A story should have a beginning, a middle, and an end. A how-to writing will have a sequence of steps. A persuasive writing has an opinion and supporting reasons and facts throughout.

As you discuss the ways to organize different types of writing, be sure to share examples from books. I find it helpful to use picture books or short nonfiction books. You're able to show the whole organizational structure in a short amount of time. Read some of your favorite books aloud. Help kids give a name to the organizational techniques they notice. Chart structures as you go or have kids take notes in their writing journals.

Arranging letters to form words, our words to form sentences, and our sentences to form paragraphs is a progressive set of skills. In addition to organizing an entire piece of writing, we can look at how to organize information within the writing. For example, a paragraph would have a topic sentence and supporting details. This first lesson is all about constructing a paragraph (unless you're teaching a lower grade level where a paragraph may be the entire story or piece for them!).

Following the lesson, you can expand with the next lesson, to show how the paragraphs can be combined to construct an entire essay.

Recipe: A Paragraph Has Legs

Notes from the Chef

Anytime we can give a visual as a pneumonic device, it can help kids remember a concept. A chair or table is a perfect analogy for a paragraph. You need to have at least three or four legs to support it. The tabletop or chair seat needs to have those supporting legs, just as a main idea in a paragraph needs to have some supporting sentences.

Ingredients

Set of sentence strips: There should be one sentence with a main idea and the other four with supporting details.

Chair

Tape

Appetizer

Put kids into groups of four or five students. Give each group a set of sentence strips. Example sentences could be:

Then you need to organize them by the events you want to scrapbook.

There are a lot of steps involved with scrapbooking.

It takes a lot of time to keep up with a scrapbook, but it is worth the effort.

Last, you need to come up with creative ways to display the photos and decorate the pages.

First, you need to print off all of the pictures you are going to use.

Ask students to work together to put their sentence strips in order on the table in front of them. Discuss how they decided the order. Was it tempting to put the sentence that says, "First" first? Or to put the sentence that says, "Last" last? Why wasn't that correct? How did you know how to *organize* them?

Cooking Demonstration and Practice

1. Discuss what a paragraph is. A good paragraph starts off with a main idea sentence that lets the reader know what it's going to be about.

2. Tape the first sentence strip, "There are a lot of steps involved with scrapbooking," onto the top of a chair or stool. This is telling us what we are going to read about: the steps involved in scrapbooking.

3. Next, tape each supporting sentence to a different leg on the stool. These sentences support the main idea, just like the legs support the seat of the chair. They go into more detail about the main idea.

4. Model writing a main idea sentence about your students' specials schedule, or something else they can all relate to. Write it down and set it on the seat of a chair. An example could be:

   We get to go to a different specials class every day.

5. Brainstorm supporting details that could go onto the legs to support that idea.

6. Example supporting sentences could be:

> It's fun to learn new songs in music and make things in art class.
> Gym class is like having an extra recess and I learn to type in computer class.
> You can get a new book in library class.

7. Come up with a "wrap-up" sentence to conclude your paragraph:

> I'm glad we get to do something "special" every day.

8. Assign each group of students one of their specials classes. Have them write a main idea sentence and supporting details to go with their class.

Dessert

Have someone from each group share their paragraph about their assigned specials class. Did their "leg" sentences support their main idea?

Recipe: A Paragraph as Part of a Patio

Notes from the Chef

This is just pushing the analogy a bit further—from a chair at the patio to the entire set! Now we're looking at putting paragraphs together for an entire essay, report, or story.

Ingredients

Picture of an umbrella table with chairs

Paragraphs from previous lesson

Appetizer

1. Project a picture of an umbrella table with chairs. Show how each of their "specials" paragraphs could be a chair at the table (main idea on the seat and supporting details on the legs). One chair could be the paragraph about music, another could be the chair for art, and so on.

2. Discuss how the umbrella could represent an introductory paragraph that covers what the whole essay is about. Together, craft an introduction about their specials classes.

3. Share that you now have an introduction, supporting paragraphs, and need to wrap it up with a conclusion. The tabletop and legs could represent the wrap-up paragraph that covers what the supporting paragraphs included. Write a conclusion for your essay.

Cooking Demonstration and Practice

In groups of four to five students, assign each group a paragraph for an essay about what they learn at their grade level. One group could write the introductory paragraph, another group could write about the subject of math, another reading, another writing, and another could write the concluding paragraph.

Dessert

When students have finished, piece them all together for a unified essay and project it up and/or read it aloud. Make any improvements as a group.

Organizing Fiction Writing

Kids may not be aware of all of the different ways that stories can be organized. For example, you could share some of Jan Brett's or Laura Numeroff's stories that have full-circle structures. You could read one of Lisa McCourt's *Stinky Face* books, which are organized around a dialogue between a mother and her son. Kevin Henkes's book, *Wemberly Worried,* follows a problem–solution structure. Wemberly has a worrying problem that we see her work through.

For the youngest writers, you may simply make a beginning, middle, and ending graphic organizer or planner for a story. Fold a piece of paper lengthwise into thirds to create three sections. The kids can open each flap to jot a few details of what will happen in the beginning, middle, and end of their stories.

For more experienced writers, students can use a traditional story plot arc graphic organizer to detail the exposition, rising action, climax, falling action, and resolution. Or they can use a planner for the character motivation, inciting incident, multiple attempts and failures, and ultimate result. In this section, we will look at ways to organize personal narratives and fiction writing. We can plan out how to organize our stories and also look specifically at each part of our stories: the beginning, middle, ending, characters, and setting.

Recipe: Two Rectangles + Four Squares Planner

Notes from the Chef

This is an easy planner to use with younger kids to plan a story that is only four to six sentences long. It is also a great planner for older kids to plan a story with four to six paragraphs. You can use it accordingly.

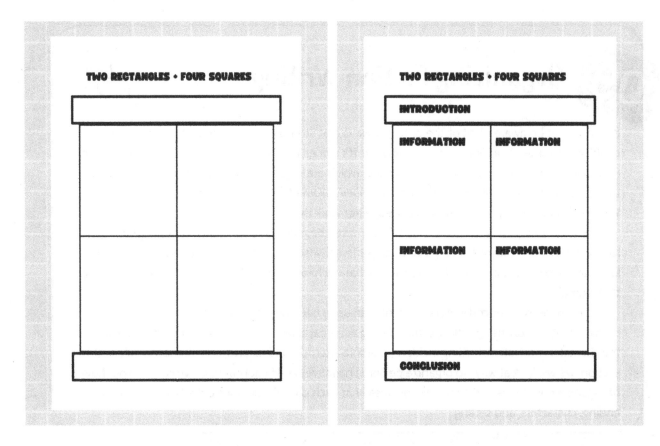

Ingredients

Two Rectangles + Four Squares Planner

Appetizer

Discussion: When organizing a piece of writing, we have some kind of beginning, or introduction. The writing in the middle is organized into chunks of information, or paragraphs.

We also have some kind of conclusion at the end. Using Two Rectangles + Four Squares is a way to "shape up" what we're going to write about. How could we use these shapes to plan what we want to write? Show example with the shapes labeled.

Cooking Demonstration and Practice

1. Model writing a personal narrative. Choose something from your ME Page, or use the example here to talk through how you would plan your personal narrative.

TWO RECTANGLES • FOUR SQUARES

WOOF! WOOF! WOOF! WE BROUGHT HOME A NEW PUPPY!

PICKING OUT THE PERFECT PUP	PICKING OUT A NAME
• Lots of pet stores • Lots of breeders • Animal shelter • Looking at ads	• Don't want to use the name of other dog • Ideas from everyone • Searching online • Voting
TEACHING HIM NEW THINGS • Potty training • What he can and can't chew • Where he has to sleep	**NEW THINGS WE MUST LEARN** • Don't leave the gate open • Don't leave shoes out • Go for lots of walks

RUDY IS A LOT OF WORK, BUT I WOULDN'T TRADE HIM FOR ANYTHING!

2. Be sure to brainstorm and talk aloud as you figure out the introduction, what to say in each paragraph, and how you would wrap it all up. Be sure to point out that besides the beginning and the ending, you are not using complete sentences. These are just notes.

3. Ask students to choose a topic from their ME Page. Pass out the planner PDF to fill out.

4. Allow plenty of time for students to fill out ideas on their planner. Have students save these for a future writing assignment when they will actually write out their narratives.

Dessert

Students will not be writing their narratives today. This is just showing them an efficient way to plan. Demonstrate using your planner to orally tell what your story may say once complete. Allow students to partner with someone to orally tell their story, using their planners.

Recipe: Narrative Beginnings

Notes from the Chef

The beginning of a story is a big deal. From an author's perspective, we want the beginning to hook the reader in and cause them to want to keep reading. From a reader's perspective, you want to get a feel for the tone and type of story it is.

You want to feel grounded in some way or have your curiosity peaked. There are several ways you can do this. This lesson will share all kinds of ways we can begin our stories.

Ingredients

Plate, cup, utensils, napkin
Mentor narrative texts with different types of beginnings
Chart paper
ME Page

Appetizer

Set a table in your room with a place setting: plate, cup, utensils, and napkin. Ask a student volunteer to knock on the classroom door and pretend they are coming to your house for dinner for the first time.

1. You answer the door and whisk the student off to the table, set them down, put the fork in their hand, and say, "Eat!"

2. The student will probably be a bit confused at this abrupt behavior, and rightly so. Share with the class that we wouldn't welcome someone into our house for dinner like that.

3. Have the student knock on the door again. This time you may have other volunteers act as your spouse, kids, dog, or others in your home. When you answer, invite them in the door and welcome them. Introduce them to your family. Show them around. Then walk them to the table. Maybe even ask what they'd like to drink.

4. This time, you've introduced your guest to some "characters" and the "setting." You gave them some grounding before jumping in to the main course. This analogy is like our stories. We want to introduce the readers to something. We can welcome them into our story with the characters, setting, or many other things before hopping into the main events.

Cooking Demonstration and Practice

1. Gather 5–10 books with different beginning lines. Read each beginning and have students decide what the author was using as a technique or introducing the reader

to. Record each on chart paper as you go. Here are some example books I use year after year:

> *Verdi*: "On a small, tropical island, the sun rose high above the steamy jungle." (Setting)
>
> *Me First*: "Pinkerton was pink, plump, and pushy." (Character and alliteration)
>
> *Bridge to Terabithia*: "Ba-room, ba-room, ba-room, bariptiy, baripity, baripity, baripity–Good. His dad had the pickup going." (Onomatopoeia)
>
> *Coasting Casey*: "Casey, please pay attention!" says my teacher, Mr. Tay. Oops! He caught me drifting off... .It happens every day. (Dialogue)
>
> *Charlotte's Web*: "Where's Papa going with that ax?" (Question)

2. Have kids go to their seats to retrieve a book they are currently reading. Let some students share the beginning lines of their books. Discuss which type of beginning the author used. If they're not already on the chart, add the new types of beginnings.

3. Project up your ME Page, from the beginning of the year. Allow a student to pick a topic from it. Then allow a student to choose three different beginning techniques from the chart you just created. Using the chosen topic, model writing the three types of beginnings the student chose. Think aloud as you figure out your three different beginnings.

4. Have students get out their ME Pages and choose a topic. On three separate pieces of paper or documents, have students craft three different beginnings.

Dessert

> Allow several students to share their favorite beginning out of their three examples. Have students save these beginnings in their writing folders for future use.

Recipe: Which Is the Real Intro?

Notes from the Chef

> This lesson is a great way to have kids practice writing a beginning and assessing the beginnings others write. It is gamified, as students are trying to trick classmates into believing that their beginning is the one written by the author.

Ingredients

> Mentor text that students aren't familiar with
>
> Enough lined paper for all students
>
> Whiteboards and markers for students
>
> Optional: prize for the winner

Appetizer

Show the cover of an unfamiliar book. (You can do this activity with any or all genres.) Have kids think about what the introduction to a book like that might say. Explain that you're having a contest to see who can get the most points. They can earn five points for guessing the actual introduction by the author, or get two points for each time other students guess that their written introduction is the correct one.

This activity causes kids to use the higher-order thinking skills of judgment and evaluation. They not only have to discern while trying to write a professional-sounding introduction but also when hearing the writing of others.

Cooking Demonstration and Practice

1. Have each student craft a two- to three-sentence introduction for the book.

2. Collect all of these digitally or on paper. If you have them write on paper, be sure to write the actual introduction on identical paper. Mix up all of the introductions and number them from one through however many intros you have.

3. Have students come back to your sharing area with a whiteboard and a marker.

Dessert

1. Read aloud each beginning and its corresponding number. Students who believe an introduction might be the real one can record the number of the intro on their boards.

2. After reading all of the intros, take a show of hands for how many people voted for each one. If the intro doesn't get at least 10 votes, it is taken out of the contest. This should significantly narrow down the selections.

3. Reread the few selections left and have students record their final vote on their boards for which number they think is the real author-generated introduction.

4. Tally up the points for each student.

5. Pass out some small prize or celebrate the person who earns the most votes in some way. (I used to staple an oatmeal cream pie packaged snack to a thick ribbon and use it as a "medal" to put around their neck.)

Recipe: Crafting Endings

Notes from the Chef

There are many ways to end a story. We want to be sure to close all of the open loops and satisfy the reader. There are many ways to do this. We can end on a fun surprise or a discovery or celebrate a character's triumph. Let's look at different ways we could wrap up our stories.

Ingredients

Plate, cup, utensils, napkin

Mentor narrative texts with different types of endings

Chart paper

Mentor book students haven't read

Appetizer

Continue the role play of the dinner scene from the narrative beginnings lesson. Have a student sit at the table with the place setting. This time, you are pretending it is the end of the meal. The student should pretend to be eating.

Take the fork out of the student's hand and swiftly walk them to the door and say good-bye. This is an example of an abrupt ending that doesn't finish in a satisfying way.

Role-play the scene again. This time, ask the student if they want some dessert. Then ask if they want to join you in the living room to visit more. Next, walk them to the door, sending them off with an extra slice of pie. This is an example of an ending that *is* satisfying.

Make the analogy of how sometimes our endings seem abrupt and leave readers feeling like they are missing something. It's important to tie up loose ends and end on a good note.

Cooking Demonstration and Practice

1. Prepare an anchor chart to record example endings. Share the endings of various books that use different techniques. Many may be repeats of the techniques used in beginnings. Mentor texts I like to use include:

   Tackylocks: "Tackylocks was an odd bird, but a nice bird to have around." (Character)

   Verdi: "Leaping and looping with his little striped friends, Verdi laughed." (Alliteration)

   If You Give a Mouse a Cookie: "And chances are, if he asks for a glass of milk, he's going to want a cookie to go with it." (Full-circle ending)

   I LOVE Strawberries!: "I Love Blueberries! I love them so much I could eat them everyday! Mom. . ." (Cliffhanger)

   Some students may realize that some of the ways we begin and end a story use the same techniques.

2. To practice writing an ending, read a picture book the students haven't read yet. Stop right before the climax/ending and have them choose a technique from the chart to craft an ending for the book.

Dessert

Choose several students to share the endings they wrote for the book. After reading the student examples, read the actual ending of the book for the class.

Recipe: The Mighty Middle of a Story

Notes from the Chef

So many times, we get kids to write a beginning and come up with a challenge for the character, but the character solves it much too quickly. This leads to a short and possibly boring story. We have to create situations for our character to fail or stumble many times. This gives them a chance to grow and learn. It also adds tension, causing us to care about what is going to happen.

Ingredients

One Day, The End, by Rebecca Kai Dotlich
I LOVE Strawberries! by Shannon Anderson
Chart paper
"Somebody, Wanted, But, So, Then" foldable organizers

Appetizer

Read the book *One Day, The End*. This book has beginnings and endings and no middles. Read a few examples and share how "boring" these stories are. The problems are solved way too easily and quickly. We don't care about the characters or what happens because we don't get to know them at all. We need to know a character and their goals and problems to care about them. Once we care about them, we want to see them reach their goals and solve their problems.

Cooking Demonstration and Practice

1. Choose a story with a character who makes multiple attempts to solve their problem or meet their goal. I like to use *I LOVE Strawberries!* Show the "Somebody, Wanted, But, So, Then" chart. Go through each part and fill it out in front of students to go along with the book.

Somebody- Who is the main character (the <u>somebody</u>)?

Wanted- What did the character <u>want</u>?

But- <u>But</u> what made this difficult?

So- <u>So</u> how did the character deal with the conflict?

Then- <u>Then</u> how did the story end?

Somebody–Jolie

Wanted–She wants to be able to grow her own strawberries in a patch.

But–

1. Her parents say she has to be older because it's a lot of work.
2. Her parents say they cost a lot of money.
3. Her parents say they don't know where to plant them.

So–

1. She tries to look older by drawing wrinkles on herself. She also shows she can handle the work by taking care of her bunny and some grass seeds.
2. She has a lemonade stand to help raise money for the plants.
3. She finds a place in the yard to plant them.

Then–Her parents see she is responsible enough and let her grow her own strawberries.

1. Pass out the foldable organizers. Have them create a character and write it under the "Somebody" flap. Under the "Wanted" flap, have them write something the character wants to accomplish. For the "But" flap, have students think of several ways the character meets obstacles. For the "So" flap, write the ways the character tries to solve the problems and trials. For the "Then" flap, students will share how the character finally meets their goal or solves their problem.

Dessert

Have students orally share their story with a partner, using their notes in their foldable organizer.

Recipe: Story Spine Technique

Notes from the Chef

I learned this technique at a writing conference in a picture book craft session. Everyone in the room was able to come up with a story in a short amount of time using this technique. I now use it when I teach picture book workshops. This formula can help kids come up with a storyline pretty easily too.

Ingredients

Mentor text: *Penelope Perfect*, by Shannon Anderson

Appetizer

1. Ask kids to share some of the things they do on a "normal" day. What are some of their routines or habits?

2. As you read *Penelope Perfect*, discuss what Penelope's normal routine is for the first half of the book.

3. When the thunderstorm happens, Penelope is forced out of her routine. Explain that this is called an "Inciting incident." It is when something happens that sets the story moving in a different direction.

4. A series of events happen after the inciting incident that eventually create a new "normal" for Penelope. Discuss the events and how Penelope is different at the end.

Cooking Demonstration and Practice

The story spine technique uses a series of sentence starters to help writers create a plot for a story. The sentence starters are as follows:

Once upon a time. . .
And every day. . .
Until one day. . .
And because of that. . .
And because of that. . .
And because of that. . .
Until finally. . .
And ever since that day. . .

1. Write the sentence starters on an anchor chart. Call on someone to make up a character. It can be a person, animal, monster, alien, or whatever they'd like. Ask for a few details about the character or setting to add. Maybe they pick a spider.

2. Ask students for something that is a normal day or habit for the character. Maybe every day, the spider has to put on and tie his eight white shoes before he goes to school.

3. Ask a student to provide an inciting incident. What happens that keeps the spider from wearing his white shoes?

4. Have students contribute ideas for the three things that happen because of this. Maybe he has to wear a different color of shoes or no shoes at all. Maybe he has to save money to buy new shoes.

5. Come up with the climax. What finally happens that relieves the tension?

6. Come up with the spider's new normal. Maybe the spider realizes that dark shoes hide stains better or that it is easier to spin webs with no shoes at all. What does the spider do from that day on?

7. Put students in pairs. Have them go back and forth with the sentence stems to create a basic plot of their own. One student will choose a character, the other will create that character's "normal," and so on.

Dessert

Choose a few student pairs to share their story spine stories with the class.
Be sure to save these stories for a later day when you are ready to add more details and elaboration.

Developing Characters

When we read a story, we picture the characters in our minds. We develop feelings for them. Sometimes we care deeply about them. Other times, we want them to get what is coming to them. This makes a difference in how invested we are in the plot. It makes us want to keep reading to see what will happen.

When characters are well-developed, we can imagine what they're going through. This is the goal when we're writing a story. Whether the story is a personal narrative about the writer or a fictional story about a talking monster, we want to write in a way that helps the reader know both the characters' physical traits as well as their personality traits.

There are many ways we can add some authenticity to our characters. We can play around with the points of view to practice getting into our characters' minds. There are also ways we can get to know our characters as we develop them. This section will help writers to be mindful of the thoughts and actions of the characters they write about.

Recipe: Playing with POV

Notes from the Chef

We like to have kids consider other people's points of view. In this exercise, they are forced to take on the reactions of various people or animals. Socially it is a lower risk because the student isn't sharing their own opinion; they are taking on the persona of what was given to them to portray.

Ingredients

Slips of paper that each say one of the following: Zebra, Lion, Giraffe, Penguin, zookeeper, zoo veterinarian, elementary kid, parent, and so on (enough slips of paper for each student to have one)

Slips of paper that each name a specific person, their age, and a brief description (for example: "Dr. Kidz, 38 years old, pediatrician," "Gina Frosting, 26 years old, gourmet cupcake shop owner," "Bentley, 6 years old, first grader," "Travis Padre, 30-year-old dad of twin 8-year-olds," "Dr. Diente, 40 years old, dentist")

Appetizer

Tell students that a decision was made to close all of the zoos in the state. The animals are going to be released in various countries into their natural habitats. If this were to happen, what would be the reactions of the people and animals who live in, work in, or visit these zoos?

Draw out one of the slips of paper and share a humorous or serious possible response from that person or animal's point of view. For example, if you draw the giraffe: "*What?* I'm not going to be hand-fed fresh romaine leaves at 2:00 every day by cute little kids? It's the highlight of my day! Do you know how many pictures they take with me to remember our special time together? Africa is *hot!* I won't have water misters to cool me off when it gets muggy. Speaking of water. . .will I have to drink out of the muddy streams? Ew! And wait! There won't be large fences to keep the lions away from me. Am I supposed to sleep with one eye open so I don't become Larry's late night snack? This is horrible!"

Put kids in small groups and give them one of the other pieces of paper. Allow each group to share their person's or animal's point of view.

Cooking Demonstration and Practice

1. Tell students that for their writing practice today, they will each get to come up with a reaction for a new law that is being passed. "After careful study, the United States Food and Drug Administration has determined that sugar is causing too many health issues and is being banned." (Remind them that they are writing from the point of view of the person on their slip of paper, not their own personal reaction.)

2. Pass out the slips of paper with various people on them. Direct students to write their reactions to the sugar ban from their person's point of view.

Dessert

Choose several responses that do a nice job of capturing the point of view of their designated person and share them with the class. Discuss how point of view changes with a person's perspective.

Recipe: Switching POV

Notes from the Chef

This lesson encourages kids to be creative with character personalities. If a story is told by the protagonist, they may switch it to the antagonist. This would slant the story to what that character is thinking and feeling. It can be comical.

Ingredients

Mentor Texts:

- *The True Story of the Three Little Pigs*, by Jon Scieszka
- *The Three Little Pigs*, by various authors
- The Steck-Vaughn *Another Point of View* series, by Alvin Granowsky (These are flip-over books. One example is *The Little Red Hen*, which becomes *Help Yourself, Little Red Hen!* when you flip it over.)
- *Voices in the Park*, by Anthony Browne

Appetizer

1. Make up a story about something that happened between you and another person. Maybe it is a disagreement you had with your child. Talk about what your side of the story is and what your child's side of the story is. Discuss how when we look at each person's "side," we are taking on their perspective. Stories are often told from one perspective. It can be interesting to look at how things would change if someone else in the story were to share what happened from their angle.

2. Read *Voices in the Park*, a book about a walk in the park, told by four different characters. It takes on four perspectives.

3. Discuss how the story completely changed, based on who was telling it. Why did it change? What was different? What did the author have to think about to write different versions of the same walk?

Cooking Demonstration and Practice

1. Spread out various mentor texts, such as *The Three Little Pigs, The True Story of the Three Little Pigs,* and some of the *Another Point of View* Steck-Vaughn flip-over series. Allow kids time to enjoy various examples.

2. Have students choose a story from their writing folder that they have already written. (If you have not had students write a complete story yet, you could either read aloud another story or allow them to choose a story or book to use.)

3. Have them rewrite the story from another character's point of view.

Dessert

If you read aloud a story for all students to rewrite in a different point of view, choose two or three students to share their versions. If they each chose their own story, it could take a while to read the original story and then their version. You may want to allow them to do this with a partner.

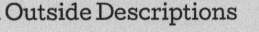

Recipe: Inside and Outside Descriptions

Notes from the Chef

When we ask kids to tell us about their characters, they often think of the physical description only. They may say it is a blonde girl wearing a pink dress, a white dog with black spots, or a furry purple monster. To fully develop a character, we also need to decide what they are like on the inside. What is their personality? What are their passions and flaws? This helps readers connect with and care about the characters in their stories.

Ingredients

Understanding Characters Chart Paper

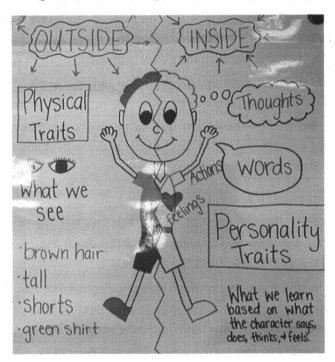

Several mentor texts with well-known characters:

Don't Let the Pigeon Drive the Bus, by Mo Willems
Fancy Nancy, by Jane O'Connor
Stand Tall, Molly Lou Melon, by Patty Lovell

Appetizer

1. Show students your character chart and discuss the difference between physical and personality traits. Add the physical traits to the left and some personality traits to the right.

2. Show the covers of several books with well-known characters, for example:

> *Don't Let the Pigeon Drive the Bus*
> Ask: What does Pigeon look like? What does he act like? What does he like and not like?
>
> *Fancy Nancy*
> Ask: What does Nancy look like? What does she act like? What does she like and not like?
>
> *Stand Tall, Molly Lou Melon*
> Ask: What does Molly look like? What does she act like? What does she like and not like?
>
> Aside from the illustrations, how do we know what the characters are like? Why do we want to know what happens to Pigeon, Nancy, and Molly? Why do we care about them?

Cooking Demonstration and Practice

1. Have students think of a character they would like to develop for a fiction story and sketch them in the middle of a large piece of paper. Have students name the character.

2. Like the chart paper, have students divide the character in half and label the left side "Physical Traits" and the right side "Personality Traits."

3. Have students write the physical traits of their character on the left side and add these details to their sketch accordingly.

4. Have students write the personality traits they want to give their character on the right side of the page. You can prompt with things like:
   - What does your character like to do?
   - What does your character try to avoid?
   - What does your character enjoy?
   - What is something your character is afraid of?
   - What is a goal for your character?
   - What possessions are important to your character?
   - Is there a flaw or habit your character has?
   - Is there something your character says a lot?
   - What personality trait gets your character into trouble sometimes?

5. Have students share these for a future story writing assignment when you are working on plot development.

Dessert

Put students into pairs and have them interview each other as if they were the character. Use the question prompts from the lesson as well as any other questions students want to add. For example, if a student named their character Kevin, they would be responding as if they were Kevin. The other student may ask them, "What are your hobbies, Kevin? What are you afraid of? What is a time you did something really embarrassing?"

These will be made-up answers, of course, but will help students think about what they want the personality of their character to be like.

Recipe: Setting the Setting

Notes from the Chef

Setting is a backdrop for where and when a story takes place. It helps us to picture the time period and place the story is happening. For this lesson, the focus will be mostly on the physical place where a story happens.

Ingredients

Large, blank piece of paper for each student
Orphan Island, by Laurel Snyder

Appetizer

Over a couple of weeks, read aloud the story *Orphan Island*. Encourage kids to keep a notebook with them as they listen to sketch new parts of the setting as you read. They will eventually have a map of the island. My students have loved this book and the island where it takes place. Before I used this book to teach setting, I had kids creating settings on Minecraft on their own at home and bringing screenshots in to share with me in class!

Cooking Demonstration and Practice

1. Allow students to share their maps of Orphan Island. What is it about the setting descriptions that helped you picture the various places on the island in your head? How did the setting help you understand what was happening in the story? What was your favorite part of the setting? What did you not like about it? What would you change? What did the characters like about the setting?

2. Allow students to get one of their stories out of their writing folder. (This can be a finished or unfinished story.) Have them think about the setting of the story the characters would be in. With the blank piece of paper, allow students to create a map of the story setting.

3. After hearing the setting from Orphan Island and making a map of their own, students may have some ideas for descriptions they could add to their own settings. Have students go back into their story and add some details. They can use a caret or tape on a "spider leg" to the spot they want to add information.

Dessert

Allow a few students to share the map of their stories and a setting detail that they added to their story for the lesson. Have students keep these in their writing folders to use as a start for a future story.

Organizing Informational Writing

Students need to know how authors organize and plan nonfiction writing. For example, in *What Do You Do With a Tail Like This?* Steve Jenkins and Robin Page start with a brief introduction, then ask about an animal's body parts, answering what each is used for as they go. It wraps up with back matter about the animals.

You can also pull newspaper and magazine articles to show how topics can be broken up and explained. You could share how-to's (organized by steps), biographies (organized by the timeline of someone's life), compare and contrasts (organized by specific features), or even problem–solution structures that take an issue, dissect it, and arrive at some solution. There are many others. The point is for students to realize that there are many ways to plan out their writing.

Just as in fiction writing, we can share lessons to hone their skills in writing good beginnings, middles, and endings. Following are some examples.

Recipe: Informational Beginnings

Notes from the Chef

When we are writing nonfiction, there are different approaches to crafting a beginning. Beginnings could include a startling fact, a definition, a quote, a question, a dramatic appeal, or a fun fact. It is somehow introducing the reader to the topic in an interesting or intriguing way.

Ingredients

Nonfiction mentor texts and magazines with different beginning examples
Chart paper
Expert List

Appetizer

Collect various nonfiction books, magazines, and articles. Share beginning lines of several, just like in the narrative beginnings lesson. Record the different types on a chart. I like to find examples of shocking statements, interesting facts, quotes, definitions, questions, and the like.

Some great resources include *Time for Kids*, *Scholastic News*, *Ladders*, *National Geographic Kids*, biographies, and various high-interest science books.

Cooking Demonstration and Practice

1. Get out your Expert List and allow students to choose one item from the list. Then have a student choose three different nonfiction techniques for beginnings.

2. Write three different nonfiction beginnings based on their choices. Think aloud as you write.

3. Have students get out their Expert Lists and choose three different techniques from the chart. Students should craft three different beginnings on three different pages or documents.

Dessert

Choose several students to share their favorite beginning lines. Have students save these in their writing folders for future use.

Recipe: Research Writing

Notes from the Chef

Some people say research is boring, but I think it's fun! If you provide access to credible sources, the hunt for good information can be exciting. Kids who are interested in their topics will want to learn all they can about it. In this lesson, I share a fun way for kids to organize all of the information as they find it. This allows them to be freed up from the management of all of the random facts. They can focus on gathering as much as possible and let the file system work its magic to create instant content for their paragraphs.

Ingredients

File folder and six envelopes for each student
Stapler
Monthly calendar

Appetizer

Show kids a typical calendar month. Ask them what they notice. Why are the squares in rows? Why are they numbered? What are calendars for? Discussion should include the fact that they are a way to organize your time. Show them your lesson plan book. Why do you have to use it? What are other examples of plans? How can we organize our writing? Why do we need to plan what we will say?

Cooking Demonstration and Practice

1. Introduce several writing graphic organizers. You could show the "Somebody, Wanted, But, So, Then" foldable (see Chapter 9). Maybe you have a Beginning, Middle, and End foldable for younger students. You could share a five-paragraph essay organizer or a Two Rectangles + Four Squares Planner (see Chapter 9).

2. Open a file folder and staple three envelopes on each side. You could label the first envelope "Introduction" and the last one "Conclusion." Show the kids how each envelope could contain information needed to write about a topic.

3. Demonstrate by choosing an animal. You could label the remaining envelopes: "Habitat," "Life Cycle," "Diet," and "Fun Facts." Demonstrate writing facts about the animal on notecards and putting them into the corresponding envelopes. In this way, all of the information they learn is organized as they go.

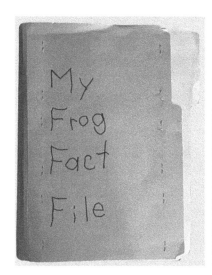 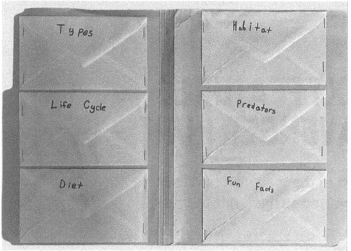

4. Have students choose an animal to research. Show them websites and books they can use to find facts about their animals. Allow them to create a file folder with envelopes and label them like you labeled yours.

5. Your focus is teaching organization, so they are just fact-finding and recording these facts on cards to put in the envelopes. Save these for an upcoming lesson on transitions.

Dessert

Allow several students to share their favorite facts and explain which envelope they filed them in.

Notes from the Chef

When we read nonfiction, the text features give us helpful visuals to guide our understanding. These may include maps, photos, diagrams, timelines, graphs, charts, a glossary, table of contents, and more. They are bonus material and a break from all of the text. In this lesson, kids will learn about the various text features and collect examples.

Ingredients

Anchor chart
Magazines, newspapers, and books with text features that can be cut up
Scissors
Glue
Scavenger Hunt List

TEXT FEATURES SCAVENGER HUNT

Find each of the following text features in books, magazines, or other text.

italicized word	title	index

 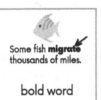 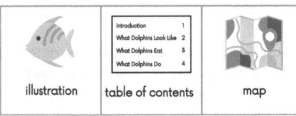

heading	chart	bold word	illustration	table of contents	map

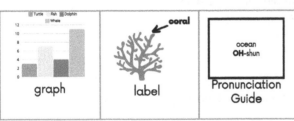 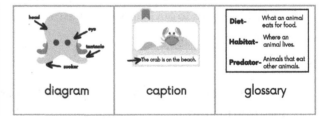

graph	label	Pronunciation Guide	diagram	caption	glossary

7	2		5	4
8	1		6	3

Appetizer

What are text features? List as many text features as possible on an anchor chart and define each one. Cut out examples from various sources and glue by each one.

Cooking Demonstration and Practice

Pass out the Text Features Scavenger Hunt PDF to students. Allow students to find as many of the text features as possible in magazines, copied book pages, and newspapers. Kids can each create their own mini-book of text features. (Be sure they are only using sources that can be cut up.)

Dessert

Students can share their text feature books with other classmates.

Recipe: Adding Text Features

Notes from the Chef

In this lesson, students will get to create their own text features as part of an informational essay. They can use their text feature booklet from the previous lesson for ideas on what kinds of text features they'd like to try.

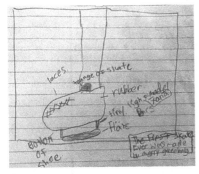
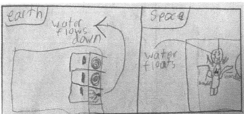
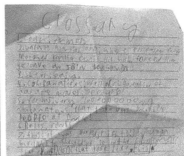

Ingredients

Text feature booklets from previous lesson

Nonfiction magazines and books

Safe-to-search websites

Expert List

Appetizer

1. Find an image of a high-interest animal to project on your board.

2. Before showing the images, try to explain the image in words. Ask students to try to repeat the information or try to sketch it.

3. Show the images. Ask students why it is now easier to remember and draw the information. Diagrams and other text features help us learn because they provide organized, visual information.

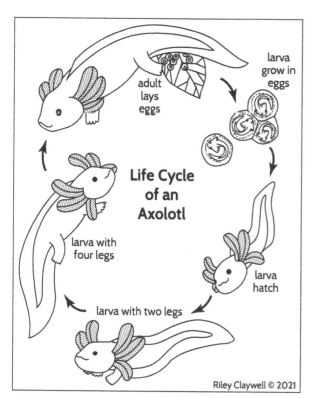

Life Cycle of an Axolotl

adult lays eggs

larva grow in eggs

larva hatch

larva with two legs

larva with four legs

Riley Claywell © 2021

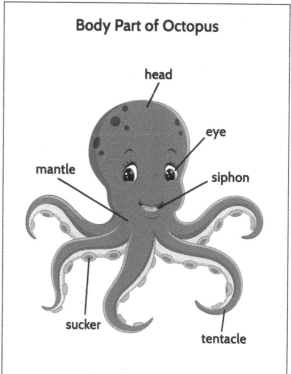

Body Part of Octopus

head

eye

siphon

tentacle

sucker

mantle

Cooking Demonstration and Practice

1. Choose something from your Expert List, an animal, or object you could explain easily.

2. Create a diagram, a map, an illustration with labels, a chart, or some other text feature. Write a paragraph about the topic. For example, if you chose the life cycle of an axolotl, you could write about that and then your text feature could be a diagram showing the cycle. If you're writing about an animal, you could write about each of its body parts and how they help it to survive. You could draw a picture of the animal and label its parts.

3. Allow students to choose something from their Expert List, an animal, or object. Let them write about that topic and create a text feature or two to go with it. If they are writing on a device, they can import photos, graphs, maps, or other features. When writing on paper, they can draw these or cut something out and glue in onto their paper.

Dessert

Allow several students to share their descriptive paragraph and text features with the class.

12 Playing with Structures

There are many different organizational structures used in books, articles, and other types of writing. This section will introduce students to some of the different ways authors organize their stories or concepts into different formats.

There are a lot of different structures! You could introduce each structure and a mentor text example and allow kids to choose one of them to try. Or you could do each one as a separate lesson. Kids could try all of the different structures if you want to spread out the lessons over days or even weeks.

Here are some to explore, along with a mentor text example you could share:

Cumulative: *My Little Sister Ate One Hare*, by Bill Grossman; *Stuck*, by Oliver Jeffers; *The Napping House*, by Audrey Wood

Parallel Story: *The Caterpillar and the Polliwog*, by Jack Kent; *Blueberries for Sal*, by Robert McCloskey

Question and Answer: *What Do You Do with a Tail Like This?* by Steve Jenkins and Robin Page; *What Do You Do If Something Wants to Eat You?* by Steve Jenkins

Diary Format: *I LOVE Strawberries!* by Shannon Anderson; *Diary of a Fly*, by Doreen Cronin; *Diary of a Wimpy Kid*, by Jeff Kinney

Letter Format: *Click, Clack, Moo: Cows That Type*, by Doreen Cronin; *Can I Be Your Dog?* by Troy Cummings; *The Day the Crayons Quit*, by Drew Daywalt

Alphabet Format: *Y Is for Yet*, by Shannon Anderson; *Z Is for Zookeeper*, by Marie and Roland Smith; *S Is for Save the Planet*, by Brad Herzog; *B Is for Belonging*, by Shannon Anderson

Compare and Contrast: *Who Would Win?* by Jerry Pallotta; *Living Things and Nonliving Things*, by Kevin Kurts

How-to: *How to Train a Train*, by Jason Carter Eaton; *Caring for Your Lion*, by Tammi Sauer; *How to Catch a Turkey*, by Adam Wallace and Andy Elkerton; *How to Walk an Ant*, by Cindy Derby

Recipe: How-to Writing

Notes from the Chef

When I taught first grade, we wrote a *lot* of how-to writings, from how to make a peanut butter and jelly sandwich to how to build a snowman. Professionally, I wrote a how-to article for *Highlights* children's magazine about how to teach your dog to jump through a Hula-Hoop. I like to explain to the kids that it's one thing to know how to do something in your own mind, but quite another to be clear enough in your instructions for another person to be able to use those steps to get the same results. I had to do a lot of research on teaching the dog this trick. I also had to test out my steps on other people to see if my steps made sense and worked when they tried the trick.

Ingredients

Various how-to articles (Several children's magazines have them.)
Recipes
Instruction booklets
How-to-draw tutorials

Appetizer

Share a recipe card on your document camera or read it aloud. Discuss how a recipe is organized. There is a list of ingredients, steps on how to make something yummy, and sometimes other things, like how many it serves or fun alterations you can try.

> Discuss what other things you could share how to do, besides cooking a favorite recipe. Things may include how to do a magic trick, how to build a snowman, how to plant flowers, or how to pack for a long trip.

Cooking Demonstration and Practice

1. Have students choose something from their Expert List. Have them decide what they could teach someone about that thing they are good at.
2. What "ingredients" would they need? What tools, equipment, or other items are necessary to teach their skill?
3. Have students number and list the steps you would take to do that skill.

Dessert

> Choose two or three student examples that may allow the class to learn something from their how-to, such as if they shared how to draw or make something. Have students follow along to see if the steps outlined are specific enough to teach the skill.

Recipe: Alphabet Structure

Notes from the Chef

> There are thousands of alphabet picture books available. Some are simply meant to teach the alphabet, but the kind I'm talking about center on a topic or theme and the alphabet is just a vehicle to share the information. For example, in my book *B Is for Belonging*, each letter of the alphabet is related to the concept of acceptance and belonging. This organizational structure allows you to write about any topic with 26 different opportunities to say something about it.

Ingredients

> Various alphabet books

Appetizer

> Read one of the alphabet book mentor text examples.

Cooking Demonstration and Practice

1. Project up or use a poster, chart, or long strip with all the letters of the alphabet on it.

2. Ask students to share concepts they learned in the book. For example, *Y is for Yet* is all about growth mindset. Kids could share things like:

   "We have brain cells called neurons."

   "We learn from our mistakes."

   "Resilience means we can bounce back and try something again."

   For each thought shared, jot the main word on a sticky note and place it on the corresponding letter on the chart. For example, "Neurons" could go on the N, "Mistakes" could go on the M, and "Resilience" could go on the R.

3. Once all the letters of the alphabet have been covered, allow students to come up and choose one of the sticky notes and let them create a page for a class book about their chosen concept. (If you have older or more advanced writers, you could have them create an entire alphabet book of their own about a topic.)

Dessert

Assemble the class book and allow students to take turns taking it home to share with their families. Include a page in the back for parent comments about the concepts and book as a whole. Once it has been through all the homes, read it aloud to the class, along with the parent comments. Then it can become a fun book for your classroom library.

Recipe: Compare and Contrast

Notes from the Chef

In my experience teaching grade levels where there was standardized testing, I found that a lot of the writing prompts were causing kids to have to compare and contrast something for example, "Read these two passages and compare and contrast the point of view of the brother in each story." Or "Read these two poems and compare and contrast the setting of the two countries." This is a type of writing that requires a knowledge of language that takes you back and forth between what is similar and what is different. Kids should become familiar with the transitional phrases that work well for this genre (see list below, in step 3). This lesson helps them practice that skill.

Ingredients

Images of similar animals (Toad/frog, bat/bird, moth/butterfly, etc.)
Venn diagram graphic organizer
Animal fact sheets

Appetizer

1. Show pictures of two similar but different animals or insects. For example, a bat and a bird, a moth and a butterfly, or a frog and a toad. Using a Venn diagram, have students help you fill out the similarities and differences between the two creatures on the graphic organizer.

2. Come up with a simple statement or question about the animals, such as "Do you know the difference between a moth and a butterfly?" This can serve as your introduction.

3. Share the different types of transition words you can use for compare-and-contrast writing. Make a list of transitional phrases and words that compare, such as:

   Just as
   Similarly
   Both
   In the same way
   Likewise

   Also make a list of transitional words that contrast, such as:

   Unlike
   However
   As opposed to
   On the other hand
   In contrast

4. Orally, have students try making a statement about how the animals are alike, using one of the transitional words or phrases. Have students try the same for contrasting statements. This will help them practice using the transitions effectively before having to write them.

5. Come up with a concluding statement about the two animals you are comparing and contrasting. For example, "Hopefully, now you have a better idea of how to tell a moth and a butterfly apart!"

Cooking Demonstration and Practice

1. Choose a different set of animals or insects that you didn't use as your appetizer part of the lesson. Because your focus for the lesson is how to write a compare-and-contrast structured writing, provide fact sheets about the animals. (You can teach them to research in another lesson.)

2. Have students fill out their own Venn diagram for the animals, using the fact sheet provided.

3. Have students compose a beginning broad statement or question.

4. Have students come up with at least two ways the animals are alike and two ways they are different. They need to write sentences using appropriate transition words in each.

5. Have students write a concluding statement or question to end their piece.

Dessert

Choose a few students to share their writing with the class, or have all students share with a partner.

Recipe: Cumulative Structure

Notes from the Chef

In this structure, elements from a story repeat and grow. A classic example of this is *The House That Jack Built*. Something continues to happen in cumulative texts and as things continue and repeat, they are often exaggerated. This can be a chance to insert some humor!

Ingredients

Mentor texts with cumulative structures:

Stuck, by Oliver Jeffers
There Was an Old Lady Who Swallowed a Fly, by Simms Taback
Song: "The Twelve Days of Christmas"

Appetizer

1. Read aloud a book with a cumulative structure, such as *Stuck*. In this book, a kite is stuck in the tree. The boy throws his shoe to knock it down. This doesn't work, so he throws his cat, a ladder, a boat, and gradually larger and larger items. It is funny because it is hyperbolic in the size and number of things that get stuck up in the tree.

2. Explain that a cumulative text has a story that builds. For example, in *There Was an Old Lady Who Swallowed a Fly*, the lady swallows a fly and then a spider and then larger and larger animals.

Cooking Demonstration and Practice

1. Discuss what cumulative texts have in common. They have a repeating phrase along with an added item or event. Play the song "The Twelve Days of Christmas."

There is a repeated line and additional gift the recipient's "true love" gives each time.

2. Model cumulative writing, such as "The Ten Days Before School Starts." You could have kids help you come up with a countdown to what a teacher does to prepare for the arrival of their students. Maybe it could start with something like:

> "Teachers get excited when school is about to begin! On the tenth day before school starts, the teacher buys one pack of postcards to send to her students. She can't wait to welcome them to be a part of the class family.
>
> On the ninth day before school starts, the teacher gets two new lunch bags one to pack her lunch in and the other to pack her lunch in when she forgets the first one at school."

> This could continue until you get to the day school starts.

3. Have students think about an event, a situation, or a problem that keeps growing. What could the repeated line be? How could they exaggerate to make it funny? Students can plan on a separate piece of paper or document. When ready, students can write their story.

Dessert

> Choose two or three students to share their cumulative stories. If time allows, they could all share with a partner.

Recipe: Diary Structure

Notes from the Chef

> I kept a diary from when I first learned how to write. I loved recording my thoughts and feelings. It was a special kind of writing that was personal and just for me. We can have a lot of fun making up what the personal thoughts and feelings are of animals or characters as a form of writing. We can also use this in the content areas to imagine what historical figures or inventors may have been thinking as they were making history or discoveries and write about those.

Ingredients

> Various diary mentor texts:
>
> *Diary of a Wimpy Kid*, by Jeff Kinney
> *Diary of Anne Frank*, by Anne Frank
> *Diary of a Fly*, by Doreen Cronin
> *Diary of a Pug*, by Kyla May

Diary of a Spider, by Doreen Cronin
Diary of a Worm, by Doreen Cronin
Dork Diaries, by Rachel Renée Russell
I LOVE Strawberries! by Shannon Anderson

Appetizer

1. Bring in a diary. Ask students if they keep a diary at home. What kinds of things do you write in it? Why do you write in it? What is the purpose of a diary?

2. Show various mentor texts with diary entries.

   Discuss what the authors (besides Anne Frank) had to think about to come up with the entries for the character.

Cooking Demonstration and Practice

1. Pick a person or animal and model writing a diary entry or two. This could be a real person, from the past or the present. It could be written about a real moment in time through the thoughts of that person. Or you could choose a fictional person or animal and imagine what they may be thinking and writing about in their diary, which could be quite humorous. For example, maybe it's a sarcastic cat who is annoyed about the dog in the house. Or it could be a zoo animal that makes fun of the people watching it.

2. Decide if you'd like students to write diary entries for a real person, an animal, or someone completely made up. Choose either a particular scenario or event to write about. This is a great opportunity for students to practice writing from a different point of view.

3. Students should write several entries for their chosen person or animal.

Dessert

   Choose a few great examples to share with the class.

Recipe: Parallel Structure

Notes from the Chef

   This is a challenging genre to write. You have to come up with a plot and share the story from two different angles or character experiences. The tricky part is in how to show the separate storylines without confusing the reader (or yourself!). This lesson gives some examples to help students see how to weave two stories together in a connected way.

Ingredients

Parallel story mentor texts such as:

Blueberries for Sal, by Robert McCloskey
The Caterpillar and the Polliwog, by Jack Kent
The Epic Adventures of Huggie and Stick, by Drew Daywalt
Finding Nemo, by Victoria Saxon
The Snow Globe Family, by Jane O'Conner
The Dog Who Belonged to No One, by Amy Hist

Appetizer

Show clips, read the book, or summarize the movie *Finding Nemo*. Discuss how there are two plots going on at the same time. We see Marlin's story of trying to find his son and Nemo trying to escape from the dentist's aquarium. This is called a parallel story because two stories are happening at the same time that are connected in some way.

Cooking Demonstration and Practice

1. Flip through the other mentor texts with parallel plots and discuss what their double plots are and how those were achieved. For example, in *Blueberries for Sal*, we see a mother and child gathering blueberries and it keeps alternating to show a mother bear and cub gathering blueberries. In *The Epic Adventures of Huggie and Stick*, both characters keep their own diary and the reader hears different sides of the same adventure. In *The Caterpillar and the Polliwog*, we see the tadpole and caterpillar going through their metamorphosis into a frog and butterfly at the same time.

2. Make a list of ways you could have plots happen at the same time. Examples could include:
   - Show what happens to one character and alternate what is happening to another character, back and forth.
   - Show diary entries of two different characters while the story unfolds.
   - Show two characters having a common problem or desire.
   - Show a character in one setting and a character in another setting going through a similar event.

3. Choose one of the examples and plot out the story. You can use chart paper with a line down the middle. Label the top of each side with a character's name. As you plot, show what is happening to both characters at the same time.

4. Allow students to choose a parallel plot strategy and create their own plot diagrams for their characters.

Dessert

The parallel plot structure is challenging and can take some time. I don't recommend having them write the actual story in this one writing block. You can do this whole lesson and stop after they have plotted. You could have students orally tell the story to a partner when they are finished. Have one or two students share theirs with the whole class. On another day, you could pull this back out to have them write out the story, if desired.

Recipe: Letters from Around the World

Notes from the Chef

I cannot tell you how much fun this project is! It is similar to the Flat Stanley project that many teachers do. Instead of sending Flat Stanley or some other character on an adventure to learn about all of the places they go, people send something directly from their location and share information about where they're from. The participants can send an item or pictures of things that are significant to their area. In their letter, they write about their state or country. We all get to learn a lot about different places around our country and the world through these packages. The beauty of it is that it turns into a research and writing project for your students as well. They do research on their own state and write a thank-you letter to the person who sent them a package.

Ingredients

Note for parents requesting letters
Stamps
Envelopes
World map
Tacks
Resources about the state where your school is located

Appetizer

1. At "Meet the Teacher Night," or in your beginning-of-the-year information, ask parents to contact one or two people who live far away and who could write to their child at school. It is awesome if they know someone from another country, but someone from another state is great too. Parents can call, email, or text these people for the initial request, asking that their senders write a letter that shares a little bit about what is significant about their state or country and what it's known for. This could be crops, sports, animals, landmarks, or famous events. If they choose to do so, they can also send pictures or an item that represents one of

these things. For example, someone from Georgia might send a small part of a cotton plant. Someone from Florida might send a few shells.

They should address their letter or package like this:

Your School Name
Student's Name ˈ Teacher Name
123 Alphabet Street
City, State, Zip Code

2. Ask students if they have ever received a letter in the mail. Chances are they have received cards, but they may not have received a handwritten letter. Why would you write a letter to someone? Possible responses include to thank someone, to share information with someone, or to request information.

3. Explain to students that your class will receive lots of letters and packages this year from different parts of the world. As your class receives mail, the recipient can put a tack on the map to show where the letter is from.

Cooking Demonstration and Practice

1. Discuss the parts of a letter: the greeting, date, body, and closing. Model writing a thank-you letter to someone who did something for you. Be sure to explain how you would be specific about what you are thankful for.

2. Model how to address the envelope and where to put the stamp and return address.

3. Provide books, brochures, websites, and other resources that have information about the state in which your school is located. Have students take notes on interesting information and fun facts about your state. Students will include this information in their thank-you letter to reciprocate sharing information with the sender about where they are from.

Dessert

Packages will typically arrive throughout the year. Allow students to open their packages in front of the class as they arrive. There should be a letter they can share telling about the state or country it was received from, in addition to pictures or relevant items for the class to see. Students are responsible for writing their thank-you letter within a week of opening their packages. Don't forget to allow them to put a pin on the map as well!

Recipe: End-of-Year Letters

I do this activity every year during the last week of school. It is a great way to reminisce about your time together as a class and all of the memories you've made. Be sure to save these letters so that future students can see them when you share them at the beginning of your next school year.

Ingredients

Lined paper

Appetizer

Ask students to help you brainstorm some of their favorite memories from the school year. Ask things like: What were your favorite projects? What did you look forward to each week? What was your favorite reward we enjoyed? What will you always remember about our class parties? What should my future students know about being in this class? What is special about this grade?

Students may say things like: I loved our field trip to _____. Our book and stuffed animal project was awesome! We got to go swimming for gym class this year. We got to do a class play. Ms. Anderson dresses funny sometimes.

Cooking Demonstration and Practice

1. Ask kids if they remember getting a letter on their desk on their first day of school. These were written by last year's students. Now it is their turn to write a letter to next year's students.

2. Model how you would write a letter about this year. Maybe it could start something like this:

   "Dear third grader,
   You are going to have a lot of fun this year! You will get to. . ."

3. Finish the letter and pass out paper to your students to write their own letters to a future student. They can refer to the chart paper for ideas. Remind them that the idea is to get the new students excited for their school year.

Dessert

Collect all of these and put them in a *safe* place for the start of the next school year. You can put them out at "Meet the Teacher Night" or on the first day of school.

Recipe: Question and Answer Format

Notes from the Chef

This is another writing format that lends itself very well to content area writing. Think of all of the material you'd like students to learn about a topic. What questions could be used to cause students to research and find the answers to everything you want them to know? It's almost like gamifying a book!

Ingredients

Mentor text with Question and Answer formats such as:

What Do You Do with a Tail Like This? by Steve Jenkins and Robin Page

Appetizer

1. Read aloud a mentor text such as *What Do You Do with a Tail Like This?* When you read it, ask for predictions to the answers as you go.

2. What other features are a part of this book? Possible answers could be: an introduction page, a pattern of questions and answers, and backmatter with more details about each animal from the book.

Cooking Demonstration and Practice

1. Use current content from something you are studying in class or allow students to choose content they could research. Be sure to provide books, safe websites, and other resources for information.

2. Model writing an introduction for a topic and one question and answer set.

3. You could have students write one question and answer set each to create a class book, or have students work individually or in pairs to create their own whole books.

Dessert

If you create a class book, allow students to take turns taking it home to share with families. If students create individual books, they could share them with students from another class, especially if the books are on a topic they are studying or interested in.

Word Choice

How can we help students make an impact with the words they choose? Part of this job is pointing out the intentional decisions of authors in other pieces of writing. When you do a read-aloud, think aloud as you notice a description that helps you picture something in your head. Show adoration for wording that makes you feel some kind of emotion. Ponder about how the author could come up with such a unique way to use various forms of figurative language.

Real writers don't normally just jot down the first thing that comes to their mind when composing something. They often make lists of words, ideas, names, and synonyms that they might use. Particular attention is paid to word choices when in the revision stages of writing. This is a time when the format and ideas of the writing are complete, but the writer wants to make their words add meaning, excitement, interest, and feeling to the page.

Recipe: Strong Verbs

Notes from the Chef

This lesson helps kids see what a difference the action words they choose can make. When we use passive or wimpy verbs, it's harder for readers to picture what is happening in their minds. Through this simple charades demonstration, kids see the point pretty quickly. Making sure we use strong verbs ensures that writing is more descriptive, precise, and impactful.

Ingredients

- Sentence strips
- Prepared writing example with passive verbs
- Mentor texts with strong verbs
- Saved student writings

Appetizer: Charades

1. Prepare five to six sentence strips with action sentences, such as:

    "She ran across the room."
    "He limped across the room."
    "She crawled across the room."
    The last one should say, "He went across the room."

2. Call on students to act out what is on the strips, one at a time.

3. When the last student tries to act out "went," he will most likely not know how to do that because it isn't specific.

4. Show the class the sentence and discuss why is was so easy to picture the other sentences in our heads, but not this one.

5. Discuss the difference between active and passive verbs.

Cooking Demonstration

1. Create a list on the board or an anchor chart with passive verbs.

2. Project your example writing on the screen.

3. Call on students to come up and cross out the passive verbs.

4. For each passive verb, brainstorm an active verb that would help us picture that action better in our minds.

5. Write each active verb above the passive verb it is replacing.

6. Have a strong verb scavenger hunt. Allow students to go through texts in the room to create a class list of strong verbs on an anchor chart.

7. Students can pull out an old piece of writing and cross out any passive verbs to replace them with stronger verbs.

Dessert

Choose four to five students to share their best verb makeover.

Recipe: Precise Nouns

Notes from the Chef

Just as strong verbs improve our writing, so do precise nouns. The same reasoning applies. Readers can picture things better in their minds and relate more to what is going on when they are given more exact details. When a writer says there is a dog running in the park, I don't picture it as well as when a writer says there is a black Great Dane running through Sprinkler Splash Pad Park. It makes a big difference, doesn't it?

Ingredients

Precise noun YouTube video: `https://youtu.be/`
`6Y-aYHr_bOQ?si=jKfPo4y0ws6ckTh7`
Precise Noun PDF
Large funnel
Paper strips with general nouns and leave many blank slips

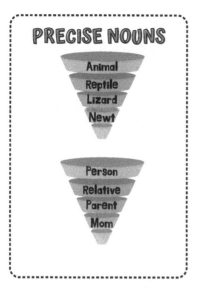
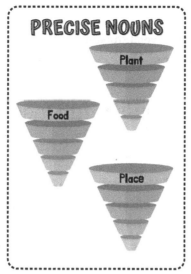

Appetizer

Show the YouTube video: `https://youtu.be/6Y-aYHr_bOQ?si=jKfPo4y0ws6ckTh7` to introduce precise nouns.

Cooking Demonstration and Practice

1. Prepare paper strips with general nouns. Examples could include Food, Person, Animal, Plant, Tool.

2. Hold the funnel and read one of the slips of paper. Slide it through the funnel. What could it be if made more specific? If you used the slip that said, "Food," you could then write one that says, "Snack." Slide "Snack" through the funnel. Write something more specific, like "Fruit." Slide "Fruit" down the funnel. What could be even more specific? Kids can name a specific fruit for the last slip of paper. Maybe they suggest a banana. Explain how this helps the reader picture exactly what the person may be eating. We can picture a person eating a banana.

3. Project the Precise Noun PDF or run it off back-to-back to show how we can funnel down nouns. We can take a very general noun and make it more and more precise.

4. Go through the examples and allow students to complete the three funnels on the next page. Ask students to use the top noun in a sentence for each one. Draw a line through the general noun and write the most specific one above it. How does that help the reader?

5. Allow students to go through their writing folders and find a piece of writing. Challenge them to find a few spots where they used general nouns and have them draw lines through them. Have students write a specific noun above them.

Dessert

Allow several students to share their noun makeovers from their writing with the class.

Recipe: Vivid Descriptions

Notes from the Chef

When a writer does a good job describing scenes and characters, readers can picture them in their minds. Why do we want readers to be able to do this? It makes writing come alive. Many people love reading because it takes them on an adventure in their minds. You get to live vicariously through the character. Your experience is more vivid and immersive if we can relate to what is being described. I have a different experience if someone says they are eating candy compared to when someone says they are sucking on a lemon drop. I can taste it with the character because I know what that is.

Ingredients

Book: *Stand Tall, Molly Lou Melon*, by Patty Lovell
Paper and clipboards if not seated at tables or desks
Markers, pencils, and crayons
Image of a target

Appetizer

1. Discuss how we can think about picking just the right words like aiming for a bull's-eye on a target. The better we describe something, the closer the reader is to being able to visualize that image in their minds.

2. Use sticky-notes to cover the main character on the cover of the book *Stand Tall, Molly Lou Melon*. When you read the book, do not show any of the pictures.

3. Tell students you will be reading a story aloud about a character named Molly. As they listen to the story, they can try to picture what she looks like in their minds. They can take notes and sketch as you read.

4. Read the story and then allow students to show their drawings of Molly Lou Melon. They usually do a great job depicting her because the author does a nice job describing her physical characteristics. Reveal the cover for students to see.

Cooking Demonstration and Practice

1. Draw a target on a marker board with an arrow to the side. Read aloud this sentence: "The bike leaned on the side of the porch." Have a student draw the bike from your sentence. Move your arrow closer on the target where you think it belongs.

2. Then add a detail and read again, "The blue bike leaned on the side of the porch." Move the arrow accordingly if the student colors the bike blue.

3. Add another detail: "The rusty blue bike leaned on the side of the porch." As the student's picture changes, move the arrow closer to the target.

4. Add another detail: "The rusty blue bike leaned on the side of the porch, tired from carrying its two passengers." Hopefully, with this sentence, the student figures out that it is an old tandem bike. Keep adding details until you have helped them reach the bull's-eye.

5. Have students do the same activity with a partner. One student will write a sentence describing a character or object, while the other draws it. The writer will continue to improve their sentence and move the arrow toward the bull's-eye as the sketcher gets closer to what the character or object looks like. If time allows, let them switch roles and repeat the activity.

Dessert

Allow several students to read their finished sentence and allow the partner to show their finished, accompanying sketch.

Recipe: Sensory Details

Notes from the Chef

One way we can bring our stories to life is by adding sensory details. We can almost hear what is going on when onomatopoeia is used. We can feel the prickly ropes in our hands when our character is swinging under the tree if it is described. Sensory details help us experience the story in a bigger way.

Ingredients

Mentor text: *Supermarket*, by Kathleen Krull
Objects for the five senses, such as sweet or salty foods to taste, textured objects to feel, noisemaking items to hear, fragrant items to smell, and interesting objects to see

Appetizer

Ask students to name the five senses. Pass out something like a chocolate candy to each student and have them write a few words to describe how it tastes. Do the same with a pretzel or cracker. Hide a squeaky toy or bell and make noise with it. Have students write down what it sounds like. Allow students to smell a flower, vanilla, or soap and describe the smells. Continue with sight and touch.

Cooking Demonstration and Practice

1. Discuss why it's a good idea to include sensory details in our writing. What does that do for the reader?

2. Share the cover of the book *Supermarket*. Ask kids which opening line helps you feel like you are in the supermarket:

   "I walked in the door and got a cart."
   or
   "Magic doors whiz open and shut. Colors glow under bright white lights."
   The second choice is the actual beginning of the book. It helps us picture ourselves walking into the store. We can "hear" the doors whiz and "see" the glow of the lights.

3. About midway through the book read, "A sweater is handy in the frozen foods section, where the air is coldest. Zippy music makes some people hum along or dance right in the aisle." This gives us details about sound and touch.

4. Model writing a sensory description of a place in the school. (The cafeteria allows for more smell and taste opportunities.) You could describe what you experience as you walk in and take a tray and take your first bite of lunch.

5. Allow students to choose a place at school or at home for which they could give a sensory description. Challenge them to fit in at least four of the senses.

Dessert

Choose a few students to share their descriptions with the class.

Using Figurative Language Devices

Figurative language is a tool that writers can use to express something in a creative way or add emphasis. There are many types of figurative language devices, including alliteration, similes, onomatopoeia, hyperbole, personification, assonance, metaphors, and idioms.

Using figurative language can help make comparisons, add humor, and paint a picture in a reader's mind. Allow students to try out different devices and add them to their writing work throughout the year.

Recipe: Let's Alliterate!

Notes from the Chef

Alliteration is probably one of the most familiar figurative language devices. You will see it when reading many picture books. It is also very easy to use in our writing. It may seem like a little thing, but this technique adds some zip to our writing because it is fun to read words with repetitive sounds.

Ingredients

A dozen or more tongue twisters, printed out
Mentor books with alliteration examples in them
Let's Alliterate! PDF

LET'S ALLITERATE!

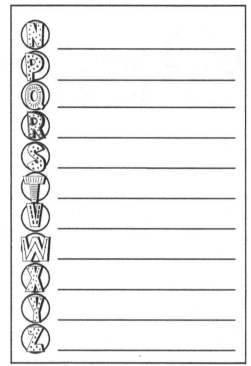

B _____
C _____
D _____
F _____
G _____
H _____
J _____
K _____
L _____
M _____

N _____
P _____
Q _____
R _____
S _____
T _____
V _____
W _____
X _____
Y _____
Z _____

Appetizer

Collect and print a dozen or more tongue twisters. Pass them out to students to read aloud. Ask students what they notice. Why are they called tongue twisters? How would you create one? If you have a die with letters on it, have a student roll it and then create a tongue twister on the board or an anchor chart in front of them using that letter.

Cooking Demonstration and Practice

1. Alliteration can be described as the repetition of beginning consonant sounds in a phrase or sentence. Find examples of alliteration in various books to share with students. Define alliteration and discuss how it helps to add some "flavor" to writing by creating a fun reading experience.

2. Share examples from books:

   Me First, by Helen Lester, page 1: "Pinkerton was pink, plump, and pushy!"
   Discuss the ways this is more interesting and attention-getting than saying, "Pinkerton was pink, large, and bossy."
   Too Shy to Say Hi, by Shannon Anderson, page 9: "I'm lucky to have three buddies with feathers, fins, and fur."
   Discuss the ways this is more interesting and attention-getting than saying, "I'm lucky to have a bird, a fish, and a dog."?

3. Pass out the Let's Alliterate! PDF. Ask kids to write a phrase or sentence for each letter.

Dessert

Ask students to choose their favorite line of alliteration to share with the class or a partner. This page can be saved in their writing folders as a reminder to try alliteration in their writing when appropriate.

Recipe: Noisy Words (Onomatopoeia!)

Notes from the Chef

Who doesn't enjoy a good, noisy word? Adding words that help us "hear" what is going on definitely makes the reading more interactive. It is also great fun to get to make up words for the sounds they represent. One of my favorite onomatopoeia examples is in the book *Verdi*. On page 27, Verdi is falling down from a tall tree branch and the author describes the sound of him hitting the branches on the way down. "Whippety, whappity, fwip, fwap, WHAM!" How fun is that to say? And it adds some action to the description of him falling. Encourage kids not only to use this device, but also try making up new ones of their own. They get to invent fun words!

Ingredients

Mentor books with examples of onomatopoeia, such as:

The Great Fuzz Frenzy, by Janet Stevens and Susan Stevens Crummel
Verdi, by Janell Cannon

Appetizer

1. Define and discuss what an onomatopoeia is. You can explain that it is a word that mimics a sound. You can share examples such as Honk! Buzzzzzz! Slurp! Hisssss! Why do writers use onomatopoeia? How does it make us feel more a part of the story?

2. Read a book such as *The Great Fuzz Frenzy*.

3. Have students write down the onomatopoeic words they hear as you read.

Cooking Demonstration and Practice

1. Create a chart with the "noisy words" students heard in the book you read aloud.

2. Have students do a scavenger hunt to find more onomatopoeic words. Provide at least a dozen picture books with lots of examples in each. They can add to their lists they started from the read-aloud and also add to the class chart.

3. Students can choose a piece of writing from their writing folders to add this device to.

4. Model how you would choose a sentence that could benefit from a sound word in a piece of writing. For example, in this passage, you could focus on the spots where sounds could add sensory details:

   > **Before**: I couldn't wait to eat breakfast. I was *so* hungry. Bacon and eggs, here I come.
   >
   > **After**: Crack! Crack Crack! Sizzle Sizzle! Mmmm! I couldn't wait to eat breakfast. I was *so* hungry. Bacon and eggs, here I come. Chomp!

5. Have students redo a passage in one of their writing pieces. They can use their "Noisy Words" list for inspiration.

Dessert

Allow a few students to share their onomatopoeia before-and-after makeovers. Be sure they keep their Noisy Words list in their writing folders for future use.

Recipe: Best Hyperboles in the Entire World!

Notes from the Chef

Kids are naturals when it comes to exaggerating. Sometimes writers exaggerate to add some humor. Other times it is to add effect. It may help someone realize the exasperation a character is experiencing. For example, if a character is being pestered by a sibling, he might say, "For the millionth time, *stop it*!" Or maybe someone has more homework than they think is fair. Instead of saying their bookbag is heavy, they might say, "My bookbag weighs a ton!" These expressions help us to feel what the character is feeling, so it makes the story relatable.

Ingredients

Best Hyperbole PDF

Mentor books with hyperbole examples, such as:

Llama Destroys the World, by Jonathan Stutzman
I LOVE Strawberries! by Shannon Anderson

Appetizer

Define and discuss what a hyperbole is and why it may be used. You can share that it is an exaggeration used for emphasis or humor. Share a few examples of hyperboles from mentor books, such as:

Llama Destroys the World, pages 13–14, after Llama rips his pants: "The rip was thunderous. It shook the house, the trees, and the mountains." This example shows hyperbole used for humorous effect.
I LOVE Strawberries! page 15, while Jolie is waiting for an answer from her parents: "Mom and Dad have been talking in low voices for like 100 minutes!" This example shows a hyperbole used for dramatic effect. It didn't really take 100 minutes, but it *felt* like that to Jolie.

Cooking Demonstration and Practice

1. Model writing some hyperboles for students. For example, if you wanted to share how tall someone was, you could say, "He was so tall the giraffes were jealous!" Or if you wanted to say that someone was very old, you could say, "She was so old, she probably rode a dinosaur to school when she was a kid."

2. Pass out the "Best Hyperbole" PDF. Kids will fill this out with their own unique hyperboles. As they are filling it out, choose responses from student's papers to use for a "Mad Libs" type of activity.

3. Once you have gathered a response for each blank, project up or read the following passage. (This does not use any hyperboles.)

    > Yesterday, I woke up in the middle of the night, shivering. My heater went out. I couldn't fall back to sleep. I called the maintenance guy to fix my heater. Then my sister stopped by. She brought her loud dog over for me to babysit. Today will be nice when my house is warm and quiet.

4. Next, read the passage with the student responses in the blanks:

    > You would not believe how yesterday started. I woke up in the middle of the night, shivering. My heater went out. It was *so* cold, _____ _____. Then I couldn't fall back to sleep. I tried _____ _____, but that didn't work. I called the maintenance guy to fix my heater. He took so long to get there that _____ _____. I think it's because he was old. I have a feeling that back when he went to school, _____ _____. Then my sister stopped by. She brought her dog over for me to babysit. I would rather _____ _____ than watch her dog. It was so loud that _____ _____. Today will be nice when my house is warm and quiet. It will be better than _____ _____.

5. Discuss how the hyperboles added humor and entertainment to the passage.

Dessert

Have a hyperbole contest. Who can exaggerate in the biggest, funniest way? Give students the following prompts to hyperbolize:

> She was very messy.
> It was so disgusting.
> He was so boring.
> Allow students to share their best hyperbole with the class and cast votes for the favorites. You could make buttons or awards that say something like "Best Exaggerator in the World!" or "The World's Best Hyperbolizer!"

Recipe: Personification Stations

Notes from the Chef

Personification is an engaging way to emphasize a nonhuman's characteristics by giving them human qualities. It could be an object, an animal, or even a concept. If we say a story jumped off the page, we know that a story can't literally jump. However, this saying lets us know that it must be an active, lively story to be described that way.

Ingredients

YouTube video: "What Is Personification?" https://youtu.be/D8X-a3SO5 Xo?si=oVgMAaR1DeYz0jOC

Appetizer

1. Tell students that you will be asking for a definition of personification after they watch the YouTube video "What is Personification?".

2. Ask students to define personification. Why would we use it? You can explain that it gives life to objects or animals, making them act, feel, or talk like humans. It goes beyond describing an object. It is more engaging and creative when you bring an object to life through personification.

Cooking Demonstration and Practice

1. Set up and introduce various Personification Stations. You can do as many stations as you'd like and decide how many students you want working at each station. Have some kind of signal or sound to let students know it's time to switch to the next station.

Station 1: FIND IT!

Students search through books, poems, and song lyrics to find and record personification examples they find. Examples include:

The Giving Tree, by Shel Silverstein, pages 1–3: "There once was a tree. . .and she loved a little boy."

Coasting Casey, by Shannon Anderson, page 10: "My pen has a mind of its own."

Come on, Rain! by Karen Hesse, page 7: "The smell of hot tar and garbage bullies the air." Page 12: "A breeze blows the thin curtains into the kitchen then sucks them back against the screen again." Page 14: "Trees sway under a swollen sky, the wind grows bold and bolder." Page 16: "The first drops plop down big, making dust dance all around us."

I LOVE Strawberries! by Shannon Anderson, page 18: "The clock moved soooo slowly." Page 24: "My strawberries are going bonkers!" Page 26: "My berries loved the rain." Page 28: "I think the patch is getting tired."

Station 2: DRAW IT!

Give a few personification examples that would be easy/funny to illustrate, such as:

> The cupcake was calling my name!
> The plant begged for water.
> The sun kissed my skin.

Students can either illustrate your given examples or create their own to illustrate. These can be done on plain paper or in their writing notebooks.

Station 3: MAKE IT!

Gather various objects such as a marker, book, fork, shoe, box, eraser, and the like. You could also have pictures of bigger objects such as a chair, fan, clock, sled, and so on. Students can refer to one of the objects or pictures to make their own personification examples. They can record these in their writing notebook.

Station 4: MATCH IT!

Have cards with things, cards with actions, and cards with locations. Have students match them up in ways that create personification examples. (They must be grammatically correct.)

> "Things" could be:
>
> > The flowers
> > The story
> > The engine
>
> Actions could be:
>
> > Danced
> > Invited me
> > Choked and coughed
>
> Locations could be:
>
> > In the grass
> > To another world
> > At the stoplight

Station 5: THE WEATHER STATION!

Using weather-related words, students will create personification examples. List as many weather-related words as possible to spark ideas: raindrops, thunder, lightning, wind, tornado, sunshine, dew, hail, snow, heat, cold, ice, fog, and so on.

> Students can record these in their writing notebooks.

Dessert

You can choose a few student examples to share, or allow students to display their favorites on their desks/tables and let kids walk around to admire everyone's work.

Recipe: What Is Assonance?

Notes from the Chef

This is a literary device that I didn't know much about until I was an adult, to be honest. I had read and heard sentences with assonance in them, of course. But, although I knew the language sounded nice, I couldn't really put my finger on why. This is a more subtle technique that should be pointed out to students, even if just to show the intentionality that goes into choosing words for a sentence. That alone can help kids see that words are thoughtfully planned by writers.

Ingredients

Mentor books with assonance examples
YouTube video: "What Is Assonance?" `https://youtu.be/V3dbb9Yulpc?si=E5XmFdpUAP03OAWk`
A copy of the poem "My Puppy Punched Me in the Eye," by Kenn Nesbitt

Appetizer

(Note: This lesson may be better suited for upper elementary.)

1. Show the YouTube video "What Is Assonance?".

2. Define and discuss assonance. Explain that it is the use of repeated vowel sounds in a phrase or sentence. Why would authors do this? What effect does this have on readers?

Cooking Demonstration and Practice:

1. Use one or two examples from books with assonance in them, such as:

   Everything You Need for a Treehouse, by Carter Higgins, page 17: "You'll be glad for the stack of snacks you stashed in your backpack."
   Page 18: "Red licorice and drippy peaches are my favorites but if you like pistachios, those are okay, too-"

2. Ask students which vowel sounds they hear repeated in the examples. What does this tell you about what writers think about as they construct their sentences? How does this make it more poetic and memorable? How is this different than alliteration?

3. Project the following poem:

My Puppy Punched Me in the Eye
by Kenn Nesbitt
My puppy punched me in the eye.
My rabbit whacked my ear.
My ferret gave a frightful cry and roundhouse kicked my rear.
My lizard flipped me upside down.
My kitten kicked my head.
My hamster slammed me to the ground and left me nearly dead.
So my advice? Avoid regrets;
no matter what you do,
don't ever let your family pets take lessons in kung fu.

4. Have students find examples of both alliteration and assonance through-out the poem.

5. Model writing a sentence using assonance.

6. Have students try composing a sentence with assonance.

Dessert

Choose a few great student examples of assonance and allow the students to share them.

Recipe: Similes Are as Easy as Pie!

Notes from the Chef

Similes are a fun substitution for adjectives used alone. It is using the words "like" or "as" to compare two things that have something in common. This comparison usually uses a noun that is being compared to another noun that is known for a particular quality. If the cashier is taking a long time, instead of just saying the cashier is very slow, you could compare them to something else that is known to be very slow, such as saying that the cashier was as slow as a sleepy sloth. We know sloths are slow, so we understand that this cashier must be taking a really long time to do their job!

Ingredients

Mentor books with similes in them
Prepared simile starter stems
Simile Starter PDF

Similes

A figure of speech comparing two different things using "like" or "as"

Complete the simile starters:

- I am as happy as a _____
- He is as fast as a _____
- She is as tall as a _____
- My friend is as sweet as _____
- I was as cold as _____
- The dog was as playful as _____
- The cat was as brave as _____
- The turtle was as shy as _____
- The shark was as scary as _____
- His feet were as big as _____

Appetizer

1. Read a mentor book with lots of similes, such as:

   Muddy as a Duck Puddle, by Laurie Lawlor
   Crazy Like a Fox, by Loreen Leedy

2. Discuss what a simile is and why you would use them. How does it help us picture a scene or character in our minds? How does it make your writing more interesting?

Cooking Demonstration and Practice

1. Have students get out a sheet of paper and number it from 1 to 5. Share aloud five simile starter stems for students to finish on their papers. Prompts could include stems such as:

   I was as hungry as
   I was as busy as
   I was as lazy as
   It was as green as

It was as sticky as

It was as bumpy as

The dog was like a

He was clueless, like a

She was smart, like

2. Go through each one and have kids share their responses. If anyone has a similar response to someone else, they have to cross out their response. Read off the unique responses that are left and allow students to vote for the most creative ones for each.

3. Pass out the Simile Starter PDF. Remind students that similes are best when they are unique and creative. Have them complete the similes on the page as a reference to keep in their writing folders for future use.

4. Have students choose a piece of writing from their writing folder. Students need to find an adjective on the page and turn it into a simile. For example, if they said that they were tired, they could use a simile to expand their description. "I was as tired as a track star at the end of a long race."

Dessert

Allow a few students to share their sentence makeover with the class.

Recipe: Making Metaphors

Notes from the Chef

Metaphors are very similar to similes in that they compare two things that share similar qualities in some way. This technique does not use the words "like" or "as." Metaphors can be used to evoke an emotion better than using a simple adjective. If the classroom seems chaotic, instead of saying, "The classroom seems wild today," you could say, "The classroom is a zoo today!"

Ingredients

Mentor texts with metaphor examples, such as:

Coasting Casey, by Shannon Anderson
I Am Peace, by Susan Verde
I Am the Storm, by Jane Yolen and Heidi Stemple
My Hair Is a Garden, by Cozbi A. Caberera
My Heart, by Corinna Luyken
My Mouth Is a Volcano, by Julia Cook
Owl Moon, by Jane Yolen
YouTube video: Simile or Metaphor? https://youtu.be/NSGjWYbGwNY ?si=hCLFJx5QCP5KM2CS

Appetizer

Review what similes are: comparison using like or as. Discuss what metaphors are: comparison without the use of "like" or "as". Show the YouTube video "Simile or Metaphor?" and have students stand up on the similes and sit down on the metaphors as they are shown.

Cooking Demonstration and Practice

1. Show the covers of several books that have metaphors for titles, such as: *I Am the Storm, My Mouth Is a Volcano, My Hair Is a Garden*, and *I Am Peace*. Discuss what these metaphors may mean and why the author would use them. Open some of the other examples to the pages with metaphor examples. In *Owl Moon*, on the second to last page, the metaphor is "But I was a shadow as we walked home." In *Coasting Casey*, "It's like I'm going nowhere. . .a hamster on a wheel." In *My Heart*, "My heart is a window. My heart is a slide."

2. On chart paper, record the metaphors you have already shared in the video and books. Ask students for examples of metaphors they have heard before, such as:

   "You're a real peach!" when describing someone as being grumpy

   "That person is a pig," when describing someone who is a slob or eats too much

   "You're a chicken," when describing someone who is afraid

3. Have students go on a metaphor scavenger hunt through websites and books to add to the chart. Challenge students to come up with metaphors of their own. How could you describe a person who is angry, besides being a volcano? To what could you compare a person who is very busy?

Dessert

Have students copy the metaphors into their writing notebooks or take a picture of the chart with their device. Allow several students to share any original metaphors they create.

Recipe: Idiomatic Expressions

Notes from the Chef

Idioms are expressions that may have been started years ago for some other reason, but are still used currently because the saying stuck. For example, back in the sixteenth century, the arrival of some big, important person was announced by the trumpeting of horns. The expression "He's tooting his own horn" means he's boasting about how important he is.

Idioms are like vocabulary words. There are too many to learn them all and new ones are created all the time. These are particularly tricky for English language learners. It's sort of like being on the outside of an inside joke. If someone interprets the expression in a literal way, it wouldn't make any sense at all. Teaching idioms can help these kids to understand some English-language expressions. You can have them share some idioms from other languages and cultures too!

Ingredients

Text message image

> I'm steaming right now.
>
> What has you bent out of shape?
>
> Becca doesn't have a kind bone in her body!
>
> I'm all ears. What happened?
>
> I caught her red-handed, stealing from my friend!

Various mentor books containing idiom examples

Appetizer

1. Define and discuss what idioms are. Explain that they are expressions that typically mean something vastly different than their literal definition. It can be fun to research the origins of how various idioms started. Using idioms can liven up writing and expand vocabulary.

2. Project the text message PDF. Based on the context of the conversation, ask students to guess what they think each of the idioms mean.

3. Research the origin of some or all of the idioms used.

Cooking Demonstration and Practice

1. Just like learning vocabulary words, learning idioms is never-ending. New idiomatic expressions are created all the time. Check out an idiom dictionary to share with students. Teach them how to look for the meaning of idioms online. You can have

students create their own Idiom dictionaries in which to record idioms as you go. You can even have an idiom of the week for the whole school year.

2. Place chart paper on eight separate tables around the room with the following idiom categories: Animals, Human Body, Weather, Colors, Feelings, Food, Clothing, and Sports.

3. Put students into eight small groups. Ask the groups to list on the chart any idioms they can think of or find. After a few minutes, signal for them to move to the next chart. Students have to try to add idioms not already listed by previous groups. Continue this until all groups have contributed on all of the charts. (A great resource is the Scholastic Idiom Tales book set.)

4. Students can then walk around and copy down one idiom they want to research, making sure to cross it off the list so no one else duplicates the same one. On their own paper or poster, students will write their idiom, write its meaning, write its origin, and then illustrate it.

5. Display these in the room or hallway, or allow students to share with the class.

Dessert

Choose a day students can come dressed as an idiom. Don't allow them to share what they are. It's more fun to have students take turns in front of the room showing their costume and props. Other students can guess which idiom they represent.

Adding Humor

Stories with humor are enjoyable to read. There are many techniques for adding humor, such as the way the voice of a character comes through, perhaps in the way the dialogue and situations mix to create funny conversations. Incongruities can also create humorous plots. For example, it can be amusing if a character or action contradicts something you know to be true. Maybe a character doesn't know how to use an object and uses it in a way that isn't correct. The reader knows the correct use, so it is funny. Clever use of onomatopoeia, hyperbole, or puns can also add humor.

A story can be full of humor, or may use humor only in certain parts. Both fiction and nonfiction can use humor to add levity or to release tension. Humor is a great tool to make writing more creative and fun.

Recipe: Pun-tastic Word Play

Notes from the Chef

Puns are a fun type of expression playing off of a similar sound or meaning of words. For example, saying ice cream's favorite day of the week is sundae is a play on the word Sunday. Sunday is an actual day of the week, but sundae is also the word for a treat made from ice cream. Studying puns can help kids learn about words with multiple meanings in a humorous way.

Ingredients

Pun examples (You can find a lot of them on the Facebook group Unappreciated Puns.)
Greeting cards with puns
Cardstock and/or construction paper
Large envelopes

Appetizer

1. Discuss what a pun is. Explain that it is a form of wordplay that uses terms with similar or identical sounds, meanings, or spellings for humorous effect.

2. Show several pun examples.

Cooking Demonstration and Practice

1. Puns can be tricky to come up with. One way to generate puns is to take a word and then brainstorm other words or phrases that sound close to it. Or the word could be the same word but with a different meaning or uses.

2. Model how to brainstorm puns. For example, you could choose an animal like a chicken and start coming up with as many related words and phrases as possible:

    Words that sound similar:
    Checkin'
    Chick in
    Thicken

    Related Words:
    Eggs—egg-citement, eggs-plosion egg-cellent, eggs-ercise, eggs-pert, eggs-cuse me
    Hatch—hatching a plan
    Peck—im-peck-able, peck-uliar
    Cluck—clock, luck

3. Try to come up with a riddle using some of the brainstormed ideas that could be on a greeting card. For example,

    "Egg-cited to wish you. . .an im-peck-able birthday!"
    "Wishing you the best of cluck!"
    "Eggs-perts agree that you are the best! Thank you!"

4. Create your greeting card with a sketch and share who you would give it to.

5. Allow students to brainstorm puns and create their own greeting cards. They can illustrate and color their cards.

Dessert

Allow students to give their card to someone in the school or take it home to give to a family member or friend.

Recipe: Comic Clash

Notes from the Chef

Publishers and librarians often say they love to get books that have heart and humor. One way we can add some humor to a story is to pair two things not typically associated together. This clash of our expectations and what really happens can make us laugh. Students enjoy taking something that may be a stereotype or generalization and turning it on its head.

Ingredients

Mentor texts with incongruencies, such as:

Mostly Monsterly, by Tammi Sauer
Mother Bruce, by Ryan T. Higgins
Pig's Egg, by Katherine Sully
Prudence, the Part-Time Cow, by Stephanie Laberis
Scaredy Squirrel, by Mélanie Watt

Appetizer

Discuss what it means for something to clash, like mismatched clothes. It can be funny when something contradicts, or is incongruent with what we think of as "normal." Share some of the mentor book examples and explain why they make us giggle:

- *Mostly Monsterly*: We expect monsters to be scary, unlikeable, and gross. Bernadette is a monster who likes to pick flowers, pet kittens, and bake cupcakes with sprinkles.
- In *Mother Bruce*, we think of bears as dangerous animals who eat other animals. We don't expect Bruce to start taking over as the mom of a flock of baby geese!
- *Pig's Egg* is funny because we all know that pigs don't lay eggs. But in this story, pig sees his friends goose, duck, and hen lay eggs. When he sees a turnip next to him, he thinks *he* has laid an egg.
- In *Prudence, the Part-Time Cow*, Prudence is not like regular cows who graze and drink from the pond. She is a scientist, engineer, and architect!
- *Scaredy Squirrel* is funny because we sees squirrels as daring and brave. We see them jump from roofs to tree branches. We see them run along electric wires high in the air. Scaredy Squirrel is afraid to take any risks and refuses to leave his tree.

Cooking Demonstration and Practice

1. Have students decide on a character that they could write a short story about. It could be a person or animal. Have them brainstorm things that are "normal" for that person or animal.

2. Challenge students to come up with actions the character could take that would be the opposite of what we would consider consistent with who they are. What would clash with their personality expectations? Have them make a list of examples of these things.

3. Keeping the mentor texts in mind, what kinds of problems would these contradictions create for their characters? Would they be made fun of? Would they be left out? Would other characters want to be like them? Would their silly traits cause havoc in a situation? Allow students to list these ideas.

4. Allow students to write a short story about their character and have them ramp up the humor as much as possible. Encourage exaggeration and extreme reactions.

Dessert

Allow several students who exemplified humor through clashing comedy to share their stories.

16 Making It Flow

It's possible that your students have never thought about the fluency of their sentences. In fact, some of them may be thrilled just to get down a few complete sentences. When we challenge our students to intentionally focus on the sound and flow of their writing, we're asking them to listen for smooth streams of words that are easy to follow.

Sometimes this can be achieved by varying the lengths of our sentences and the sentence patterns we use. Transition words can help writing to sound more natural as well. We can use sequential words to show the gradual passage of time. Likewise, we can use transitions to show a cause-and-effect relationship or how something compares or contrasts to something else.

One helpful way to check your writing for fluency is to read it aloud or have a friend read it back to you. This will help you hear where the words cause the reader to pause or stumble over awkward phrasing. You can work out fluency issues by trying it orally before you write it down.

Recipe: Go with the Flow!

Notes from the Chef

This lesson looks at the flow of our writing. In other words, how does it sound when it's read? One of the best ways to test writing for this is to read it aloud. To achieve fluency, the sentences typically need to be different lengths. They also need to start in different ways. Starting four out of six sentences in the same paragraph with "she," for instance, doesn't flow as well as sentences with more variety in structure.

Ingredients

"This Sentence Has Five Words: A Lesson from Gary Provost on Varying Sentence Length," `https://www.aerogrammestudio.com/2014/08/05/this-sentence-has-five-words/`

Appetizer

Gary Provost's "This Sentence Has Five Words" is an excellent example of how fluency makes a difference. Read it aloud to the kids:

This sentence has five words. Here are five more words. Five-word sentences are fine. But several together become monotonous. Listen to what is happening. The writing is getting boring. The sound of it drones. It's like a stuck record. The ear demands some variety.

Now listen. I vary the sentence length, and I create music. Music. The writing sings. It has a pleasant rhythm, a lilt, a harmony. I use short sentences. And I use sentences of medium length. And sometimes when I am certain the reader is rested, I will engage him with a sentence of considerable length, a sentence that burns with energy and builds with all the impetus of a crescendo, the roll of the drums, the crash of the cymbals—sounds that say listen to this, it is important.

So write with a combination of short, medium, and long sentences. Create a sound that pleases the reader's ear. Don't just write words. Write music.

~Gary Provost

Cooking Demonstration and Practice

1. On chart paper or the whiteboard, write several short, choppy sentences. Here is an example:

   We were hungry after dinner.
   We went to the store for ice cream.
   We picked out vanilla.
   We bought whipped topping.
   We got bananas and strawberries.
   We bought chocolate.
   We made banana splits.
   We loved them.

2. Ask kids what they notice about this example. Be sure they realize that all of the sentences are about the same length. There is no sentence variety because they all start with the word "we." It's basically a long list and lacks expression.

3. Have students work with a partner to create the same scene, but with varying sentence lengths. Encourage students to try some transition words and phrases. Have students create a variety of sentence stems. Challenge them to add some variety in emotion to add inflexion and interest.

Dessert

Allow several pairs to share their ice cream scene makeovers.

Recipe: Transition Types

Notes from the Chef

I didn't really learn about transitions until high school English class. That's a shame because elementary students are definitely capable of learning how to use them to improve the flow of their writing. We use different types of transitions for different types of writing. Teaching about each kind and practicing them can help kids get accustomed to using them.

Ingredients

Transition Types PDF

TRANSITION TYPES

ADDITION

ADDITIONALLY
FURTHERMORE
MOREOVER
IN ADDITION
ALSO
BESIDES
AS WELL AS

COMPARISON

SIMILARLY
LIKEWISE
IN THE SAME WAY
IN COMPARISON
AS WELL AS
JUST AS
BOTH

CONTRAST

HOWEVER
IN CONTRAST
WHILE
YET
ALTHOUGH
DESPITE
UNLIKE
BUT

CAUSE & EFFECT

THEREFORE
THUS
AS A RESULT
BECAUSE OF
SINCE
FOR THIS REASON
IN ORDER TO

CLARIFICATION

IN OTHER WORDS
SPECIALLY
THAT IS TO SAY
TO EXPLAIN
TO CLARIFY
THIS MEANS
TO PUT IT DIFFERENTLY

SEQUENCE

FIRST, SECOND,
THIRD
NEXT
THEN
LATER
AFTERWARD
FINALLY
IN CONCLUSION

EXAMPLE

FOR EXAMPLE
FOR INSTANCE
SUCH AS
IN PARTICULAR
TO ILLUSTRATE
INCLUDING

SUMMARY

IN CONCLUSION
TO SUM UP
ULTIMATELY
OVERALL
TO CONCLUDE
TO SUMMARIZE
AS YOU CAN SEE

EMPHASIS

ABOVE ALL
ESPECIALLY
IMPORTANTLY
INDEED
UNDOUBTEDLY
CLEARLY
IMPORTANTLY
PARTICULARLY

YouTube video: "Transitions Simplified!" `https://youtu.be/`
`pEtb9XbgJ-c?si=KPVgnfBs_b8ElfQh`

Appetizer

Show a short news clip. (Preview ahead of time to be sure it's school appropriate.) Most often, during the news, the anchor will say some kind of transition to go from what they are reporting to the weather person. Point this out. Ask students why this is better than abruptly just flashing to the weather report.

Cooking Demonstration and Practice

1. Show the YouTube video "Transitions Simplified!" This covers different types of transitions, and also talks about the need for transitions between ideas within a paragraph and between the paragraphs themselves.

2. Pass out the Transition Types PDF to students. Allow a student to pick two of the types. Demonstrate an example of using those transitions or phrases. For example, if someone chose for you to demonstrate a transition for "emphasis," you could write, "I love ice cream. Cookie dough ice cream in particular is the best kind ever!"

3. For the second one, if a student picked "clarification," you could write, "I'm an early bird. In other words, I get up before the sun!"

4. Have students choose two different types of transitions to try out. Have them write out their examples in their writing notebooks.

Dessert

Choose a few students to share their examples. Try to find as many examples from different types as you can.

Recipe: Trying Transitions

Notes from the Chef

As kids learned in the last lesson, there are different types of transitions to use for different types of writing. Here is a lesson that makes use of transitions used to persuade. A mix of transitions can be used for emphasis, to sequence, and to summarize.

Ingredients

"Adding Ooomph to Persuade" writing lesson (Teachers should be allowed to wear jeans on Fridays.)
Story Glue Poster
Sticky notes
Transitional words and phrases list

Appetizer

1. If you have already taught the Compare and Contrast lesson, remind students of the types of transitional phrases you used to show how animals were the same and different: both, similarly, on the other hand, however, and so on.

2. Discuss how there are other types of transitional words and phrases we can use for other types of writing. Transitions are kind of like "story glue" holding the story together.

3. Make or project an image of a glue bottle. Write transitional phrases that could work nicely with your "Teachers Should be Allowed to Wear Jeans" writing: For example, One reason, Furthermore, As you can see, In addition, Plus, As you can see, Clearly, Obviously, Therefore, Lastly.

4. Project up the "Jeans" writing and allow students to come up and place sticky notes from the glue bottle to the beginnings of sentences in the writing. When finished, it could look something like this:

> "Teachers should be allowed to wear jeans every Friday.
>
> You'd have to agree, having a wardrobe of fancy clothes is expensive. Teachers don't make a lot of money.
>
> In addition, people are more comfortable when they can be more casual. Elementary teachers are on the floor, kneeling next to student desks, and moving around a lot. Obviously, stretchy, casual clothes are better suited for this.
>
> Furthermore, teachers can relate to their students better when they are dressed like them. Being able to wear a class or school spirit shirt (with jeans) can unite the class. Clearly, just like a sports team, bonding with what makes us alike can be powerful.
>
> As you can see, teachers getting to wear jeans can help with a teacher's budget, help them feel more comfortable, and bond them with their students. Therefore, if they can't wear them every day, then just on Fridays would be a first step."

Cooking Demonstration and Practice

1. Pass out a writing sample that lacks transition words. It should be a paragraph or short story with many opportunities to add transitional words and phrases. Allow students to work in pairs to write in the transitions.

2. Through this lesson, students have practiced using transitions for persuasion. Through the Compare and Contrast lesson, they became familiar with transitions best suited for comparison. Another set of transition words that are commonly used are sequential words and phrases. These are used when there is a set of steps or an order to events. Examples you could list for the class include: First of all, To begin with, Next, Secondly, Then, Further, Lastly, Finally.

3. There are a number of ways you could practice sequential transitions. You could allow students to revisit their "how-to" writing lesson. They could write out their how-to directions using transitions. Another option is to read a story and have kids do a retelling of the story. As they recall the story, they can use the sequential transitions to move their retelling along.

Dessert

Choose two or three students to share their writing with the class.

Emotion

Emotion is another important ingredient in our writing. Nailing down how to achieve an authentic voice in your writing can be challenging. I like to think of emotion as what separates a long list of words from a meaningful message with purpose. Emotion can reflect mood, personality, intention, and audience. It brings energy to the page.

We not only have different voices for different audiences, we also have different voices for different kinds of writing. If we are writing breaking news for the newspaper, it's going to sound different than if we're writing an opinion piece or a thank-you card. We adjust our tone and how formal we are based on our purposes for writing.

If we're writing a story, we can have the characters use a dialogue in a way that sounds like their personalities. This helps us to get to know them better. When we're writing an informative report about the importance of gun safety, we would want a serious tone.

Recipe: Voice Role-Play

Notes from the Chef

The main consideration when we are determining our "voice" for a piece of writing is the audience who will be reading it. This lesson helps kids think about their audience and allows them to have some fun role-playing various voices.

Ingredients

Funny picture book
High-level technical or medical textbook
Biography of a famous athlete
Poem by Shakespeare

Appetizer

1. Have students imagine what type of audience will be reading the piece they are writing. For example, when I'm writing a picture book for kindergarten or first-grade kids, I imagine a six-year-old child reading or listening to the pages. I make my writing voice match how I would talk to that child or how the character would sound. I think about what they would understand, what they may think is silly, or what they feel is important. I wouldn't use a sentence like, "The mechanic was

trying to recollect the procedure to use on the transmission." A six-year-old would not understand this and would quickly lose interest or become frustrated.

2. Read a passage from a picture book, a high-level technical or medical textbook, a biography of a famous athlete, and a poem by Shakespeare.

3. Have students imagine what kinds of people would enjoy that type of writing.

Cooking Demonstration and Practice

1. Have kids role-play how they might sound when talking to different people. They may be surprised how many voices we use to say the same thing, depending on who we say it to. For example, let's say you want someone to get a marker that is now on the floor. If you were asking your mom, you might just say, "Can you please pick up my marker?"

    If you were talking to your brother, who just threw your marker for the 27th time while you're trying to do your homework, you might say, "Go get my marker!"

    Maybe your marker rolled off your desk and over by your friend's foot. You might say, "Hey, can you toss my marker back to me?"

    But what if your toddler cousin picks up your permanent black marker and removes the cap, ready to write on the wall? How would you ask her to give it back? Maybe you would say, "Give me the marker, sweetie. . .please come here. Let me see the marker... .Can I please have the marker? Put the cap back on. Don't write on anything!"

2. Come up with another scenario where you are asking someone to do something, such as asking someone to buy you something. Or maybe you are asking for help with something. Have students come up with three or four different ways to say this, depending on the people they are saying it to.

Dessert

    Allow several students to role-play the dialogues students come up with to try out different voices and tones.

Recipe: Ewww and Awww Contest

Notes from the Chef

This lesson gives students a chance to try evoking some emotions through their writing. It has an element of fun, so students are motivated to write with as much emotion as possible to get the best reactions!

Ingredients

When Sophie Gets Angry–Really, Really Angry. . . by Molly Bang

Appetizer

1. Read a short scene from a book that depicts one of the emotions. For example, you could share this from *When Sophie Gets Angry–Really, Really Angry. . .*: "She kicks. She screams. She wants to smash the world to smithereens. She roars a red, red roar. Sophie is a volcano, ready to explode."

2. Ask students to identify which emotion is being shown here. (Do not show the cover of the book until after they guess.)

Cooking Demonstration and Practice

1. Discuss how we can use emotion in a story to show how a *character* is feeling. We can also evoke emotions from the *reader*. We can write something that causes the reader to feel a certain way.

2. For this lesson, students will try to evoke emotions from their classmates. They have the choice to be in the "Ewww!" contest, where they try to create a scene that is so disgusting, everyone is saying, "Gross!" "That's disgusting!" "Ewww!"

   Or they can be in the "Awww!" contest, where they try to create a scene that is so sweet and adorable, everyone is saying "Awww!" "That's so sweet!" "Oh my goodness!"

3. Give students time to write their "Ewww" or "Awww" descriptions.

Dessert

Allow students to share their descriptions. You don't have to vote for overall "winners" for the contest. This is more about seeing if they can elicit an appropriate response when they read their work.

Recipe: Show, Don't Tell

Notes from the Chef

As an author, I have gone to countless writing conferences and workshops. I've taken many webinars and classes. One of the craft lessons they always stress is to be sure to let the reader experience the story. We can't just come right out and bonk them over the head with what characters are doing and feeling. Good writers show this through scenes and dialogue.

Ingredients

Emotions poster
The Emotion Thesaurus, by Angela Ackerman and Becca Publisi
Mentor text: *Come On, Rain!* by Karen Hesse

Appetizer

1. Display a poster or image that shows faces with various emotions.

2. Act out one of the emotions. For example, you could pretend to be reading something on your phone and act out being very surprised. You could stand up, gasp, and say something like, "Oh my gosh! I can't believe it!" Allow students to guess the emotion from the poster.

3. Allow a few students to choose an emotion from the poster/image and use dialogue or actions to show that emotion without telling what it is. Other students can guess the emotion.

Cooking Demonstration and Practice

1. Explain what it means to "show" emotion instead of just "telling" the reader what the emotion is. When we describe situations for our readers to picture in their minds, rather than naming the emotion, we allow readers to experience what the character is experiencing. This adds emotion to our writing.

2. Show the book *Come On, Rain*! On page 10, instead of just telling readers that Mamma is hot, the author says, "Sweat trickles down her neck and wets the front of her dress and under her arms. Mamma presses the ice-chilled glass against her skin." Using these sensory details helps us picture what the character looks and feels like. We can almost feel the heat. There are other great examples in this book too.

3. Show students *The Emotion Thesaurus*, which lists all kinds of emotions. Under each, you can see the emotion defined, the physical signals for it, internal sensations, mental responses, and cues for that emotion. Share a few examples. Discuss how knowing the physical or internal signals and cues could help you describe an emotion without coming out and just naming it for readers.

4. Have students create their own emotion thesaurus. This is a great tool to create and use to come up with compelling ways to describe a character's reactions and body language. You can have students each take an emotion or two and do one page of the thesaurus.

5. Students can go on a scavenger hunt through stories and find scenes where these emotions are shown in an effective way.

Dessert

When students are finished with their emotion(s) descriptions, make copies for all students so that they can all have a complete emotional thesaurus to keep in their writing folder for future reference.

18 Grammar and Editing

The teaching of grammar and writing conventions starts at the earliest of stages. Kids learn the difference between capital and lowercase letters. They learn how to end a sentence. Whether they remember these things is not guaranteed, but they are skills we do have to have our students practice.

I like the way Vicki Spandel, the author of *Creating Young Writers*, explains conventions to her students. She starts a discussion about the conventions of eating. For example, why do we use forks and spoons and eat off of plates and from bowls? How did this come to be? Why are there rules in sports? Why do we have a certain number of players on each team and why do they wear different uniforms? Why is there a limit to how much time sports are played and points assigned? What about the conventions of driving? Why are there stop signs and why do we have to drive on a certain side of the road?

Obviously, all of these conventions help us to enjoy life, in a safer, more organized way. This is also true for the conventions of writing. When we follow the rules, it keeps us organized and allows our readers to enjoy our stories.

The mechanics of our students' writing can sometimes be the most tempting thing to pounce on with the red pen. We tend to notice missed punctuation and capitalization right away. It's an easy thing to edit. However, if we can hold ourselves back, try to let that be one of the things kids learn to edit for themselves. With a little training, an editing checklist, an online spelling and grammar checker, and/or a critique partner, those little things can be fixed.

What I try to focus on instead are the things they really do need me to coach them on. If I take out my red pen and show them all of the little spots they didn't use correct spelling and capitalization, they may equate that with being a "bad" writer. My time with them is better spent helping them develop ideas, adjust tone, or improve the flow.

That being said, I do need to teach primary students how to use punctuation correctly and give them practice spelling words. I need to provide strategies to find the correct spelling and capitalization of words. They need to be able to recognize when something doesn't look right and have strategies to fix it. I also want to teach subject and verb agreement, the correct usage of irregular verbs, and many other rules that help their writing to be clearer.

Thankfully, there are tools that can help us edit our work. If students have composed on a tablet or computer, they may be able to see spelling errors with the red squiggle under them. If Grammarly or some other grammar extension is installed, this can help them spot grammatical errors.

If students are not using a device, you can provide editing checklists, but I recommend also having kids trade papers to spot needed edits for each other. In our own minds, we know what we wanted to say and how we wanted to say it. We may not even notice some of the mistakes we make. For example, read this:

After reading this sentence, you will realize that the the brain doesn't recognize the second "the."

Did you notice the second "the" when you read that? How many times have we done this or used the wrong form of a word in an email? We know the correct way to do it, but our brain doesn't catch it. Having someone else read our writing for us can help to catch these errors.

Another thing that can help with edits is to have students check for one type of convention at a time. For example, have them check the entire paper for capitalization issues in one read. Have them check punctuation in the next read. Later, they can check for misspellings. It can be overwhelming to try to spot everything in one swoop.

I have no problem with my students using their devices to check spellings and capitalizations. I use my computer to help me find correct spellings, rhyming words, and synonyms all the time. It's what real writers do. It isn't cheating or naughty. It's being resourceful and using tools.

As we do our writing lessons throughout the year, we can teach mini-lessons on convention-centered concepts. Here are some ideas for lessons:

- How to use an editing checklist
- How to use commas in a series
- How to use commas in an appositive
- How to use periods for ellipses
- How to use contractions appropriately
- How to break text into paragraphs
- How to stop run-on sentences
- How to check for consistent verb tenses
- How to punctuate dialogue

I'm sure you can think of many more, but these are a few that can be sprinkled in among other lessons throughout the year.

Recipe: Check, Please!

Notes from the Chef

An editing checklist can be a helpful tool for young writers to use. I'm pretty sure I'm not the only one who has witnessed a student reading through the checklist and checking off the items without rereading their writing as they go. They read, "I used capital letters at the start of sentences," and check the box, without even really checking. In their mind, they are thinking, *I know I should do that. I'm sure I probably started all of them with capital letters.* In reality, just like experienced writers, we sometimes make mistakes and don't notice them until we take time to deliberately check it over. Sometimes it even takes someone else checking it for us to notice our errors because we are so familiar with the piece from working on it for a length of time.

Even though students may miss some (or a lot!) of their errors when using a checklist, if they learn to use it properly, they can at least spot and correct a good number of them. Improvement of any kind is great!

Ingredients

Editing Checklist PDF

EDITING CHECKLIST

- ☑ RE-READ: DOES IT MAKE SENSE?
- ☐ HAVE I USED THE CORRECT PUNCTUATION AT THE END OF SENTENCES?
- ☐ HAVE I USED THE CORRECT CAPITALIZATION AT THE BEGINNING OF SENTENCES AND FOR IMPORTANT WORDS?
- ☑ DO I HAVE DIFFERENT SENTENCE STARTERS?
- ☐ IS MY VOCABULARY INTERESTING? DID I USE STRONG VERBS?
- ☐ DOES MY DIALOGUE SHOW WHO IS SPEAKING AND WHAT IS BEING SAID?

Mentor texts:

Francine Fribble, Proofreading Policewoman, by Justin McCory Martin
Grammar Tales series from Scholastic
Punctuation Celebration, by Elsa Knight Bruno
Punctuation Takes a Vacation, by Robin Pulver
Twenty-Odd Ducks, by Lynne Truss
Alphie the Apostrophe, by Moira Rose Donohue

Appetizer

1. Ask students why we have stop signs, stoplights, and rules about speeding. Students will most likely (hopefully) share that these help us to be safe. These rules can even save our lives!

2. Ask students if they think grammar rules can save lives too. You will probably get some giggles or eye rolls. You've probably seen the T-shirts that say, "Commas Save Lives." They have the sentences "Let's eat Grandma!" and "Let's eat, Grandma!" Use an example like this, but with one of your student's names instead of "Grandma." Explain how that one little comma makes a big difference in meaning.

3. Read aloud the story *Francine Fribble, Proofreading Policewoman*. Discuss the rules addressed as you go. Ask students how we can be our own "Proofreading Police."

Cooking Demonstration and Practice

1. Project up the editing checklist for students to see. Go over what each item refers to and how to look for it.

2. Have students take out a piece of writing that is already completed. Use an old piece of writing or create a story ahead of time that needs something corrected for each of the items.

3. Read the first item on the list: "Reread. Does it make sense?" Tell students that you are going to work through each item on the checklist, one at a time. *This is important!* You will miss many mistakes if you are trying to check and scan for everything on the list in one pass-through.

4. Reread the story aloud. If there are parts that do *not* make sense, pause and allow students to offer suggestions to clarify. Once it all makes sense, check off the first box.

5. Move on to the second item on the list: "Have I used the correct punctuation at the end of sentences?" Read each sentence and pause to see if the punctuation is correct for each one. Make corrections as you go. When it is all correct, check off the box.

6. Keep moving through the list until you have checked off every item.

7. Pass out the Editing Checklist PDF to students. Have them get a piece of writing from their writing folders that they can use the checklist on.

8. If you have time, you could have them trade their writing and check each other's. They can use a highlighter to point out anything they may have missed when they checked themselves.

Dessert

Go through each item on the checklist and have students raise their hands for each one where they made corrections. Which item did the most students need to correct? You can read the *Grammar Tales* book that corresponds to the most common errors (or another similar mentor text) and possibly do a separate lesson another day based on that specific need.

Recipe: Dialogue Done Right

Notes from the Chef

If we are writing a reader's theater or a skit, or using speech bubbles, we don't have to worry about our dialogue punctuation as much. There are no quotation marks or tags for speakers. However, in a story, we need to know how to show who is speaking and how to use proper capitalization and punctuation. It can be tricky when we interrupt a sentence with a dialogue tag in the middle of it. And sometimes it seems strange to end what someone is saying with a comma instead of a period. Here is a recipe with some rules that can be helpful as a guide when students are learning how to write dialogue correctly.

Prepare a couple of sentence strips with some dialogue examples. Glue macaroni noodles in place for every quotation mark and comma. (You can dye them with food coloring if you want to make them stand out more.)

Ingredients

Macaroni noodles (uncooked)
Marker
Glue
Chart paper
Tips for Writing Dialogue PDF

Appetizer

1. Display your sentence strips with macaroni quotation marks for students to see. Be sure to use an example with a dialogue tag starting the sentence, ending the sentence, and with various punctuation. Example sentences are given below.

2. Start with the general rule of putting quotation marks around the words a person says. As you continue sharing sentences, go through the specific rules that apply:

   • Quotation marks go at the beginning and at the end of spoken words.

   For example: "I love books!" said Shannon.

   • Use dialogue tags to show who is speaking.

   For example: Shannon said, "I collect stories."

   • Commas and periods always go inside the quotation marks.

   For example: "I enjoy writing stories," said Shannon.

   • Every time someone new speaks, you begin a new paragraph.

   "If you read a lot of books, it helps you develop a stronger vocabulary. You learn all kinds of new words!" said Shannon

   "Yes! Learning new words helps you improve your writing, too!" said Ms. Anderson.

- If you start with the dialogue tag, use a comma after the tag.

  For example: Shannon said, "I love reading."
- If you start with the quotation, use a comma before the end of the quotation instead of a period. If it is a question, use a question mark. If it is an exclamation, use an exclamation mark.

  Statement example: "You can never have too many books," said Shannon. Question example: "Are you *sure* you can't have too many books?" asked Mom. Exclamation example: "You have *way* too many books!" exclaimed Dad.
- If the dialogue tag is in the middle of a sentence, the second part of the sentence is not capitalized, because it is not the start of a new sentence. It is just continuing the same sentence.

  For example: "Class," said Ms. Anderson, "we are going to have another amazing day!"

Cooking Demonstration and Practice

1. Pass out the Tips for Writing Dialogue PDF and go back over the rules at the top, as well as the examples.

2. Give students time to complete the conversations using proper dialogue punctuation on the back side of the page independently or in pairs. Check for understanding.

3. As students finish, allow them to use sentence strips, a marker, glue, and macaroni noodles to complete a sentence or two.

Dessert

Allow several students to share their sentences and explain which rules they had to follow to punctuate their sentences correctly. These sentence strips could be displayed on a bulletin board, if desired.

19 Revising

Students may not know the difference between revising and editing. You can explain that revising is changing the way that you wrote the words. For example, you may revise how you crafted what you want to say. Maybe you decide to create a simile to replace an adjective you used. You may change the order of how you wrote something. Or maybe you want to add more dialogue between your characters. Editing, on the other hand, is looking at the mechanics of the writing. You might correct your spelling, check your capitalization and punctuation, or fix a run-on sentence.

Revising is a habit that we hope our students will start to self-regulate. I admit, once I've finished a draft of something, sometimes I just want to "be done." There are several ways we can handle the revision process that can get kids excited rather than overwhelmed.

One way to inspire kids to want to revise on their own is by showing examples of writings by past students on a project like the one you're working on in class. Be sure to give kids some space after finishing a draft of something. You wouldn't want to dive right into fixing things and risk burning the students out.

Wait a day or two to bring out the samples and have students get their drafts out as well. As you share the great things the writer did and things they could improve, your students may notice they have done some of the same things. Encourage them to take a moment to think about anything they may want to revise in their own work after seeing the samples.

Another great technique for improving your writing is through using critique partners. This is something real writers do on a regular basis. I don't know if I'd have anything published if I didn't have my critique partners!

You can have students partner up with each other in class or invite another class from a higher grade level come in to help critique. The partner should start by reading the writer's piece aloud to them. This helps the writer to hear any stumbles the reader may make on their words. It's amazing what you notice when someone else reads your work aloud.

Using the six ingredients for a good story and your rubric language, the person giving the critique can share their thoughts on how to improve the writing. You can also provide sentence stems to help with how to phrase the feedback.

IDEAS	ORGANIZATION
"I'd love to hear more about. . ."	"Your beginning. . ."
"Your focus was. . ."	"Your ending. . ."
"I learned. . ."	"Your paragraphs. . ."
WORD CHOICES	**FLOW**
"Your verbs. . ."	"Your flow was. . ."
"I like your use of. . ."	"Your transitions. . ."
"I could really picture. . ."	"The variety of your sentences. . ."
EMOTION	**GRAMMAR**
"I felt. . ."	"Your use of. . ."
"The dialogue. . ."	"Your spelling. . ."
"Your audience awareness was. . ."	"You may want to recheck. . ."

Recipe: Advise and Revise

Notes from the Chef

Giving feedback is a skill. Getting feedback is a growth opportunity. For the most growth to occur, you need to receive good feedback and be open to accepting it. This lesson allows students to see helpful ways to share improvement suggestions. It also allows them to see you modeling the humility it takes to receive and use feedback. Lastly, this is a low-stakes activity, so students don't have to fear failure if they don't do an amazing job on the exercise they are receiving feedback for.

Ingredients

Slips of paper with a different animal or object on each one (one per student)
Blank paper
Markers or crayons

Appetizer

1. On the whiteboard, pick an object or animal to draw in front of the class. If you're feeling brave, you could have kids pick what you have to draw! Set a timer for five minutes and stop drawing when the timer goes off.

2. Allow students to give you feedback on what you could add to the drawing to make it better. Then ask them what you could erase from the drawing to make it better. Finally, what could you change completely about the drawing to improve it?

3. Make the suggested changes and discuss how the feedback helped you to improve your work.

Cooking Demonstration and Practice

1. Pass out the prepared slips of paper with animals or objects on them. Assure students that in the short amount of time and preparation for this, there are no expectations for stellar art. The focus of the lesson is on how to give and get a critique, not how to draw. Set a timer for five minutes for students to draw their assigned image.

2. Pair students with critique partners. If desired and if you have appropriate devices, you can let students take a picture of their drawing before the critique is given.

3. Allow students to share with their partner first about what they could add to improve the drawing. Then have the partner share what they could remove. Last, the partner should make any other change suggestions.

4. Have students switch roles. Once both students have received their feedback, set a timer for 5–10 minutes to make the suggested changes.

Dessert

Discuss some of the changes made and which types of suggestions were helpful. How is critiquing a drawing like critiquing a story? Allow several students to share their before-and-after drawings to show their revisions.

Assessment

> "Assessment must promote learning, not just measure it. When learners are well served, assessment becomes a learning experience that supports and improves instruction. The learners are not just the students, but also the teachers, who learn something about their students."
>
> –Reggie Routman

I have always felt like we should not grade writing to have something to put on the report card. This ever-growing skill set is part of a process. Many times, as kids learn, I'll have them write parts of a story or go back into old drafts to improve them. They may abandon stories or only develop a scene for another. I try to have their writing practice focus on the specific skills I'm teaching.

At the elementary level, there are different philosophies on assigning writing grades. Some schools give grades specifically in writing, others combine writing scores into a language arts grade, and still others don't assign grades at all.

We can all probably agree that assessment in the form of formative feedback is helpful and necessary regardless of assigning grades. We can let students know how they are doing by creating a rubric. This can be a scale that shows the level of growth for each ingredient that goes into a piece.

Rubrics can be created within the classroom with the students' input, by a grade level of teachers, or by a district coach. Some schools choose to use readymade rubrics that go along with a writing curriculum or program.

Rubrics help students understand the expectations for high-quality writing. They help teachers discover needs and gaps that inform their instruction. Grade-wide or school-wide rubrics can be great tools for teachers to maintain consistency when planning professional development and future lessons.

Although formative feedback is wonderful on a regular basis, formally assessing an entire piece is not necessary more than three to five times a year. It is better to focus on skill-based lessons and practice and only have students complete an entire story, report, persuasive essay, or the like a limited number of times.

It takes a build-up of endurance and large collection of skills to be able to pull together a polished or published piece. Think of it like a performance: a lot of practices and dress rehearsals are necessary before a final production can be expected.

Recipe: Writing Review Rubric

Notes from the Chef

We can all read the same book or story and have different opinions on whether or not it is "good." There are some components to the writing that we can probably agree on, however. We can look at the six ingredients of good writing and determine if the writer used these in effective ways.

Rubrics help students understand the expectations of a type of writing when there are guidelines provided. We know we need good word choices for a story, but to what extent? We know the writing should be organized, but what does that mean? Students can look at a rubric and compare it to their writing to see where their writing is fantastic and where it may need improvement.

In this lesson, students will see why rubrics are helpful and how to create them.

Ingredients

Writing Review Poster PDF
Writing Review Rubric PDF
Pictures/images of various student desks
Student writing samples with varying levels of quality

Appetizer

1. Before or after school one day, create various scenarios showing tidiness levels of desks or lockers. Be sure there are varying degrees of at least five different levels. Take a picture or video of each. (You can use actual students' desks/lockers, or create examples from an empty one that you reset to appear at different levels of utility and neatness.)

2. Display the Writing Review Poster and show the various desk/locker images. Ask students to decide which pictures belong to which category and why. Start with the best one and work your way backward.

3. Write a brief description in each column of the chart to explain why an image would receive that rating. For example, a desk that received the top rating, "You Are Doing It!" might say:

   - Supplies organized by needed accessibility.
   - Papers are in labeled folders and binders.
   - There is no trash.
   - Only items that belong in the desk/locker are actually there.
   - Books are stacked neatly.

4. Allow students to use the completed rubric to assess their own desk or locker. Discuss.

Cooking Demonstration and Practice

1. Display a blank Writing Review Rubric and label it with one of the ingredients of writing. Maybe you could start with "Word Choice."

2. Create or use sample writings from past students to begin the discussion on what kind of rating it would receive in Word Choice. Continue with other samples until you have good descriptions for each level of "Word Choice" aptitude.

3. Move on to the next writing ingredient on a new sheet. Maybe you work on "Organization" next. How would you describe each level of Organization based on student samples and what they know? Continue this for all six ingredients.

4. Have students choose a piece of writing from their writing folder to self-assess for one of the six ingredients.

Dessert

Share a few examples where students have selected the appropriate level of competency for their chosen piece. Discuss why it received that rating.

Recipe: Rubric-Ready

Notes from the Chef

This lesson helps students become familiar with the expectations from the rubric that will be used for their writing in class. As a class, you will rate a lower-quality writing sample. This allows kids to see the minimal expectations and their corresponding scores. Then students work to improve the writing piece in groups. Rating it this time typically moves you to the mid-upper range of the rubric. Lastly, you will work as a class to bring the collaborative writing to the top rank in all six ingredients. Students will see what it takes to achieve the scores for the highest-quality writing.

Ingredients

Writing Review Rubric PDF

WRITING REVIEW

INGREDIENTS

	STUDENT				
	1	2	3	4	5
IDEAS					
ORGANIZATION					
MAKING IT FLOW					
EMOTION					
WORD CHOICE					
GRAMMAR					

Low-quality writing sample

Appetizer

1. Prior to this lesson, use the writing review pages and your own expectations to complete the Writing Review Rubric. For this one, you will just be filling out the descriptions for the levels 1, 3, and 5. I recommend starting on level 5 and working your way backward.

2. Project up the one-page rubric as well as the writing sample you have prepared. You will want to prepare this as a low-quality writing about an animal you have plenty of resources for, such as a butterfly, chicken, frog, penguin, or the like. Be sure it uses very basic word choices, has no sentence variety, is unorganized, and lacks information and voice.

3. Read the writing aloud and have students help you score it on each of the six ingredients. It should be scoring 1s, 2s, and 3s. This allows students to get familiar with the low end of the rubric.

Cooking Demonstration and Practice:

1. Ask students to help you choose different parts of the writing that could be developed with more information. For example, maybe a paragraph could be just on the life cycle of that animal. Another paragraph could be about the diet of the animal. Another might be the habitat, and so on. Put kids into groups and assign each small group one of the paragraphs to research and develop. This is a great opportunity for students to practice using a main idea and details. If you only have a few categories and other groups need something to write, one group could be in charge of the introduction and another could work on the conclusion.

2. When the groups have finished their paragraphs, type these up into one document to share the next day. When ready, project the collaborated piece and project the rubric again. As a class, rescore the writing for all six ingredients. There should be significant improvements. This will cause students to be focused on the middle and higher end of the rubric.

3. Finally, with you at the computer, guide students in figuring out ways to bump each and every ingredient to a level 5 score. This will stretch students to become very well acquainted with the highest end of the rubric.

Dessert

Read aloud the finished, polished piece with students. Discuss what they noticed about the writing as it improved. Were there any surprises? What was the hardest part? How can this help them as they work on their own writing?

Recipe: Collaborative Conferences

Notes from the Chef

Feedback is an important part of understanding where we could improve our writing. In this lesson, students will have the chance to self-assess, then have a critique partner give them feedback, then have you conference with them. After all of this, students should be able to understand areas where they could improve that specific piece and also set some writing goals for future writing experiences.

Ingredients

Writing Review Rubric

Appetizer

1. When students have finally reached a point in the year that they have a finished piece of writing, pass out a rubric to each student to self-assess their work.

2. Next, invite another class (preferably from a higher grade level) to come partner with your students.

3. Have the visiting partner read aloud the other student's writing to them.

4. The partners can then use a rubric to determine where they feel the student scored and discuss their rationale. The student can share what they gave themselves for a score and decide which score is more accurate.

Cooking Demonstration and Practice:

1. You may allow students to make improvements based on their partner's feedback and discussion.

2. Throughout the next week, call over students individually to do the same thing with them. (This could be during self-selected reading time, writing practice time, or some other time when you can devote four or five uninterrupted minutes with each student.)

3. Read aloud their piece to them, then begin discussing the score you feel they land on for each ingredient on the rubric. Ask the student what they gave themselves as a score and talk about any discrepancies between your score and theirs.

Dessert

Once you have completed scoring, ask the student to share one or two writing goals based on this writing piece. Write their goal somewhere for your records and have the student write the goal in their writing notebook as well.

Notes from the Chef

Although I only formally assessed finished writing pieces four or five times per year, I always dreaded the day I had to lug all of those papers home. I would spend hours reading and rereading and checking each thing against the rubrics as I filled them out. When students would get their writing and rubrics back, I never felt that they really received much value from the feedback. I didn't notice a difference in their writing the next time they wrote. Any growth that was happening wasn't directly linked to seeing how I scored their writing.

Then one year, when I had a student teacher, I had an idea. While she was teaching, I would pull each student aside and do a personal writing conference to go over their piece with them. This made a *huge* difference! I urge you to try it. From that week on, I never graded students' writing without the students there. Even without a student teacher, you can independently meet with every student within a week if you are intentional about scheduling. You can use self-selected reading time, writing practice time, grab a student at the beginning or end of specials, and so on. You'll be glad you did!

Ingredients

Writing rubric (whatever your class is using for whichever genre you are assessing)

Sticky notes

Assessment clipboard or some other place to record notes

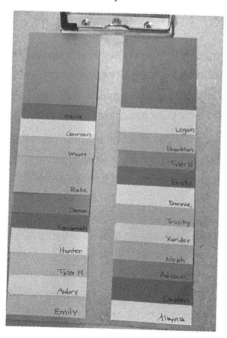

Appetizer

After students have finished a formal writing, give them a rubric to use to self-assess their piece.

Cooking Demonstrations and Practice

1. During writing practice time, self-selected reading time, or some other appropriate time, call a student over for their individual conference. You will need their writing piece and the rubric they used to self-assess. You will also need a rubric for your use to assess.

2. Resist the urge to read any of the students' writings prior to their conference. When the student is ready, read aloud their writing to them *exactly* as it is written. If they leave out a period, word, comma, or write something incorrectly, read it as they have it. This allows them to see how an audience will read their writing. I usually make comments as I'm reading. I ask questions, give compliments, and share things I'm noticing. This is giving them feedback in real time. I try not to go too far off on a tangent, because I don't want to interrupt the flow of the story or piece too much.

3. After reading and commenting, I go through each ingredient on the rubric. I start by reading the item, and I then ask the student what they gave themselves for that item and why. Sometimes, after hearing you read and your comments, they want to change their score. That is fine! (The self-assessment doesn't count as a grade anyway.)

4. After they share their score for an item, I talk through what I am going to give them for that particular ingredient and explain why.

5. After we have assessed the entire piece, I ask them what they want their writing goal(s) to be. I record their goal on my clipboard. (I have sticky notes with all of my students' names on there. I jot down a new goal each time I meet with them.) I also have the student write their goal on a sticky note. This can be put in their writing notebook or folder.

6. This process literally takes four to six minutes per student. The students learn how their writing sounds to a reader, have a chance to hear your specific feedback, and discover what they want to work on for future writings. This is *far* more powerful than just being handed back their paper with the scores on it.

7. I'm usually able to get through all of my students in one week. With all of this data fresh in my mind, I'm able to create and use focused future lessons based on the highest needs I observed during the conferences.

Dessert

In future writing block times, as I go around the room, I'm regularly checking my clipboard and monitoring students' writing to see if they are making improvements during practice time. I am able to notice and point things out as they practice and remind them of their goals if they are not yet making changes to correct their areas needing improvement.

Creative Writing Exercises

As with any subject area, we have to keep changing up the types of work our students do in writing. In math, for example, we wouldn't work on long division all year long. For reading, we wouldn't do a close reading on every text. And we have to get creative with our writing practice. These exercises not only break up the genre studies but also cause us to review skills across genres.

You can tell when your students need a breather from some intense writing work several days in a row or during an assessment period. Try out some of these short exercises to spice up their writing and have some fun. These are activities that stretch students' thinking and get them to flex their creative muscles.

Recipe: Quote-tastic!

Notes from the Chef

This lesson is good not only for thinking about alternative ways to write something but also for gaining understanding for some commonly used quotes. You can supply quotes to choose from, let kids bring in a quote, or give them time to find one in class. In order to make the quote fancier or simpler, they will need to use synonyms. They will also need to take their audience into consideration when deciding on tone and voice. This is a quickie lesson for one of those days you don't have time for a full writing block.

Ingredients

Access to quotes on a safe website or copies of quotes to choose from
Thesaurus or synonym finder website or app

Appetizer

This exercise challenges students to understand the meaning behind a powerful quote. It also causes them to play with different methods of expressing meaning, depending on the audience.

1. Share the quote "Kindness always wins."

2. Explain that a fancier version of the same quote could be "Exhibiting a warm-hearted personality will gain respect and success with friends."

3. Tell them that a simpler version of the same quote with the same meaning is "Be nice!".

Cooking Demonstration and Practice

1. Tell kids they are going to find different ways to explain quotes, based on their audience. They will pretend they have college students coming to the class. We want to impress these college kids by expressing the quote's meaning in fancy words and rich vocabulary.

2. Similarly, they are going to pretend that kindergarten students are coming to the class. They will need to take the same quote and simplify it for a kindergarten student to understand what it's saying.

3. Provide students with quotes to choose from or point them to a safe website where they can find their own. (Another option would be to introduce this one day with the expectation that they find and bring in a quote the next day to use.)

4. Once students have chosen a quote, task them with writing a fancier version of the quote and a simpler version of the quote. Allow them to use a thesaurus or online synonym finding tool for help.

Dessert

If possible and reasonable, invite high school or college students to your classroom to hear their "fancified" quotes. Allow the older students to do the same challenge of making their original quote more advanced.

If possible and reasonable, have preschool, kindergarten, or first-grade students come to the classroom to hear their simpler versions of the quotes. The younger students could illustrate the quote or share their understanding of the quote orally.

Recipe: Write It Down, Pass It Around

Notes from the Chef

Kids love writing these as much as they love reading them afterward. It is interactive and done in spurts, so it keeps students' attention. There is natural curiosity and excitement for what is being handed to them next. Then there is ownership because they get to add their own twist or details to the adventure. They can hardly wait to read each finished story to see what happened and how their part added to the plot.

Ingredients

Paper and pencils
Choose Your Own Adventure books

Appetizer

Read aloud a portion of a Choose Your Own Adventure book. (These are books that allow the reader to make choices at different stages of the story by asking if you want one thing to happen or another. Based on your choice, you will be directed to a different section of the book.) Be sure to read enough that the students get to vote for choices several times. Explain that these books are fun because readers get to decide the direction a story is going to go.

Cooking Demonstration and Practice

1. Place students in groups of four or five. Each student will need lined paper or an open document on a computer or iPad.

2. Give students four minutes to come up with the beginning of a story. This needs to include something about the character and setting.

3. After four minutes, use a sound or signal for students to pass their papers to the left. The students will read the paper they receive and then have five minutes to add to the story. They get to choose the problem for the story and write about it.

4. After five minutes, students will pass their papers to the left again. Students will read all of what is written on their paper so far and continue the story. They will more than likely be writing a way(s) the character tries to get to their goal or solve their problem. They will have six minutes to do this.

5. After six minutes, signal for everyone to pass their papers to the left again. Students will read what is developed so far and add to the story again. This will be more failed attempts to solve a problem or meet a goal. They will have seven minutes.

6. After seven minutes, have students pass their papers for a final time. This should get the paper either to the last remaining group member or the person it started with, depending on your group sizes. This last round is for wrapping up the story with a climax and a satisfying ending.

Dessert

Students typically can't wait to hear how the stories turned out. Allow students to pass their papers enough times to read all of the stories they contributed to.

Recipe: You've Got 30 Seconds!

Notes from the Chef

I always kick off any writing camps I have with this exercise. Kids will be asked to come up with key vocabulary words they would need to write about a given topic. Then you announce that they cannot use any of the words they came up with! Kids will be shocked. The point of the exercise is to impose a structure that forces them to be more creative. When you omit what is common, they have to think of the uncommon to use instead.

The only bummer is that you can only do it one time with your class. Once they know what you're going to do with the list of words they create, the surprise element is gone. (You could do it again and supply the common words they are allowed to use in their description.) These end up being quite comical to read afterward. You're sure to hear some giggles.

Ingredients

Two topics

Appetizer

1. Choose a topic and tell students they will have 30 seconds to come up with a list of key words they would need to use to write about that topic. For example, if you asked them to share how they celebrate the Fourth of July, they may want to use words like these: fireworks, Fourth of July, parade, baseball tournament, picnic, cookout, flag, and red, white, and blue.
2. Call on students and list the words they suggest. Stop after 30 seconds. Leave the list of words on the board.

3. Give them the same task with a different topic. This time, they will make their own lists on their own papers. Topic ideas could be:

> What is your normal morning routine?
> How do you make your bed?
> How does a flower grow?
> What is the life cycle of a butterfly?

4. After 30 seconds, make them stop writing and set aside their lists.

Cooking Demonstration and Practice

1. Using the list on the board, tell them you have to write about what you do on the Fourth of July, but you *can't* use any of the words on the list!

2. Students will groan or laugh. Model writing this description and think aloud as you go. Try to make it as humorous as you can to get kids excited to try the same thing. Maybe your example could read something like:

> "Each year, on the day after the third of the seventh month, we celebrate our country's independence. We like to watch a line of floats, cars, and bands go down the street. We also always play a game where we hit a sphere with a stick and run. We eat food with people and wait for it to get dark. When it's dark, we gather together to watch explosions in the sky. It's a fun day."

3. Using whatever topic you chose to have kids create their 30-second list, have them do the same thing. They have to write about the topic, but can't use the words on their list.

Dessert

Kids typically can't wait to share these. They like to get silly with their synonyms or descriptions of what they want to say without using their key words. You can choose a few to share or allow everyone to share with a partner.

Recipe: Ode to Food

Notes from the Chef

This is a fun type of humorous spoken-word poetry you can try. Have kids come up with a food they are obsessed with and let the dramatics fly! The more over the top, the better. Be sure to show the YouTube example for inspiration!

Ingredients

Ode examples

YouTube video: "A Slam Poem to Bacon," `https://youtu.be/xSVO5VloDlc?si=COqKG830NP67p-jm`

Appetizer

A true "ode" would actually follow meter rules and may rhyme. However, these odes are more related to "slam poetry," where there is free verse description, delivered with passion. These can be a fun way to get kids to use all kinds of writing elements. From figurative language to using their senses to emotional use of voice, these short pieces are powerful.

Show kids the YouTube video "A Slam Poem to Bacon," with Nick Offerman. It is a funny poem about a man's passion for the taste of bacon. Kids will crack up and see how the use of words and emotion can be fun to mix.

Cooking Demonstration and Practice

1. Choose a food you enjoy. Model writing an ode to that food in front of the students. Think aloud as you go. Start with a list of reasons you like the food. Think of sensory details and write them down. What onomatopoeia or alliteration could you tie in? Is there a spot where you could use a simile? This is also a great place for practicing hyperbole. Many spoken-word poems have rhyme. Is there a place or two where you could incorporate some rhyme? Could you add some dialogue capturing how much you love this food?

2. Have students choose a food and go through the same process. You can show them other examples of odes to food. Here is a student sample:

Spaghetti

You make me smile at the smell of your spicy sauce. The noodles. . .oh, the noodles! Slippery, delicious noodles. Mmmm! Mix them together and, yes! The perfect masterpiece for my mouth. Ribs, chicken, burgers don't really matter anymore as long as I have you, my love.

Dessert

This is best when you can have kids perform them. Are there props they can bring in? Could they wear a costume or hat with the food on it? Could they bring the food in? Incorporate as much as you can into the performance. You could invite parents or another class to watch. Or you could video kids performing their odes. It's sure to be a good time.

Recipe: Cookbook

Notes from the Chef

What kind of culinary-themed writing book would this be without having kids write recipes for a cookbook? Encourage kids to come up with a complicated recipe. It is more fun (and funny) when it's something like chicken tetrazzini rather than just a hot dog. The more they have to guess on how to make the dish, the better.

Ingredients

Recipe template PDF

Recipe for

INGREDIENTS:

_____ _____
_____ _____
_____ _____

STEPS:

_____
_____
_____
_____
_____
_____
_____
_____
_____
_____
_____
_____

Ingredients for a simple recipe that doesn't need to be cooked
Recipe card for the recipe
Food and tools needed to make it

Appetizer

Ask students what a recipe is for. How does it help us make something good to eat?

Share the recipe you brought in and make it in front of the kids. If you have a hotplate or microwave available, you may have more options than someone who doesn't. You could make no-bake cookies or yogurt parfaits. You could even show them how to make your favorite sandwich.

Cooking Demonstration and Practice

1. Allow kids to share some of their favorite foods.

2. Pass out the recipe template PDF to students and ask them to list the ingredients they would need to make it.

3. Next, have students list the steps they would need to take to make that kind of food. Be sure they include cooking time, if applicable. They can even share the temperature and how long to cook it. The more details, the better.

Dessert

Combine all of the recipes into a binder or book and allow students to take turns taking it home to share with their families. Another fun ideas is to make copies of your class "Cookbook" and let kids give them to their parents for Mother's Day or Father's Day.

Recipe: Vote for Me!

Notes from the Chef

You definitely want to do this one if it is an election year. Even if it's not, this is a fun, persuasive writing practice that shows there is a place for creative writing, even in politics!

Some schools let kids win the chance to be principal for the day. I used to do this as a chance for students to be the teacher for the day. You can specify how much the winner will actually get to do in your role. It could be that they get to sit at your desk, lead a couple of lessons, and make a few key decisions. To win this privilege, they have to run in a campaign to show they would do the best job. You could also do this for class jobs. Students would have to campaign for the class job they think they should get. Or you could do this if your school has a student council. The students who want the spot could write speeches about why they are the best candidate to represent their class.

Ingredients

Poster boards
Markers

Appetizer

Point out that even in politics, speech and slogan writers try to be creative with their words. Read or show the slogans and ask kids what kind of language device it uses. (These are in parentheses after each.) Show students these campaign slogans:

"Keep Cool and Keep Coolidge"–Calvin Coolidge (alliteration)
"We'll Buck 'em in '56"–James Buchanan (pun using last name)
"Grant Us Another Term"–Ulysses S. Grant (pun)
"Don't Change Horses Midstream"–Abraham Lincoln (idiom)
"Our Choice: Cleve and Steve"–Grover Cleveland and Adlai Stevenson (rhyming)
"Win with Wilson"–Woodrow Wilson (alliteration)
"I like Ike"–Dwight D. Eisenhower (rhyming)
"Ross for Boss"–Ross Perot (rhyming)
"Putting People First"–Bill Clinton (alliteration)
"Building a Bridge to the Twenty-First Century"–Bill Clinton (alliteration)
"I Like Mike"–Mike Pence (rhyming)

Cooking Demonstration and Practice

Depending on the type of position you want students to run for, explain what the job entails, such as Teacher of the Day, Student Council Rep, or specific class jobs. Have them use the poster boards and markers to make campaign posters.

Dessert

Allow students to share their slogans with the class. They can display their posters and/or give a small speech explaining them further.

Recipe: Stick with the Script!

Notes from the Chef

This is a favorite writing activity because staff members at the school will be using a script students write to act out for your class. Kids can't wait to put words in their mouths!

Ingredients

Props
Costumes and/or accessories

Appetizer

Pass out a short readers theater for a group of students to read in front of the class. This can be something that you create or that you find. How is a readers theater script written differently than a story? What is the format of a script?

Cooking Demonstration and Practice

1. Model writing a funny skit in front of the kids on chart paper or projected onto your whiteboard. Use the character names and a colon to show what each one is saying. (You can have a narrator if needed.) Have students help you with the lines. For example, you could do a skit of what your dog and cat say when you're coming home from school:

   Dog: *Oh my gosh! I heard the garage door! She's home! She came back!*
   Cat: Oh, calm down. She always comes back.
   Dog: I missed her so much! I can't wait for her to get in here and pet me and talk to me in that voice she uses just for me. She loves me so much and I love her.
   Cat: You are so annoying.
   Dog: Aren't you excited to see her? She's probably going to tell us all about her day. I can't wait to hear all about it! Maybe we'll get to go for a walk too!
   Cat: Your breath stinks.
   Dog: Here she comes! She's unlocking the door! *Oh my gosh!* Let's go! Aren't you going to come to the door with me to jump up and down?
   Cat: Unless she has catnip, I'm staying right here.
   Dog: Suit yourself. *Mooooooooooooom! I missed you!*
   Mom: Who's a good boy? You're such a good boy. Who wants a treat? I missed you, sweet boy.

2. Choose a couple of students to read the skit parts.

3. Place students into small groups and challenge them to write a funny skit that you will have staff members act out for them. (Check with the staff members ahead of time.) You can give them topic ideas like these:

- Teachers trying to understand some of the slang words kids use and misusing them themselves.
- Staff members telling about the best and/or worst parts of their jobs: janitors talking about cleaning up vomit, principals getting treats for kids' birthdays all the time, teachers having to grade papers after school, the PE teacher getting to wear sweats every day, and so on.
- Staff members making fun of each other. Maybe one does amazing bulletin boards or none at all. Maybe one is known for a certain habit or thing they wear. Maybe someone looks like a celebrity. Is a teacher known for being very nerdy or preppy?
- Teachers at staff meetings. What do they think and say to each other? What do they say about the students? What do they say about the principal?
- Staff members after the kids leave school for the day. What do they do? What do they say? Are they sad or excited? What do they do in their classrooms?

Dessert

Once students are finished writing their skits, allow them to present them to the class. Take a vote for which one(s) you will ask staff members to come and act out for your class. They will love seeing the adults at the school being silly because of the words they make them say in their skits!

Recipe: I Didn't Know That!

Notes from the Chef

It's always fun to learn unbelievable facts, but even more fun when you get to share them with others to see their reactions.

Ingredients

Mentor texts with fun or amazing facts, such as:

Ripley's Believe It or Not
5000 Awesome Facts (About Everything!) by National Geographic
Interesting Facts for Curious Kids, by David W. Leon
Amazing Sports Stories for Kids, by Eli Spark
The Fascinating Science Book for Kids (500 Amazing Facts!) by Kevin Kurtz
The Ultimate Book of Random Fun Facts, by Bill O'Neil

Appetizer

Find a few shocking or amazing facts that seem unbelievable to share with kids. Chances are that your students will want you to expand and share more about each one. This is exactly the kind of excitement and engagement we want! Explain to kids that if they find a cool, unbelievable fact, others will want to hear all about that too. Fun facts are entertaining and educational. Today's writing will be the chance to find fun facts and share them with others.

Cooking Demonstration and Practice

1. Pass out the fact books you have collected and allow students to pore through them. Chances are, you may have to give them lots of time because these are generally high-interest and kids want to keep reading.

2. Ask students to each choose a fun fact that they want to research further. They can use the information in the book they found it in as well as information found in other sources. You may need to provide safe websites students can use to find more information.

3. Students will research and write up their findings in a one-page document or page. Challenge them to really give their fun fact some spice by playing up their title. Maybe they can begin with "Did you know that. . ." or "You are not going to believe this, but. . ."

Dessert

You can allow students to each share their fun fact or create their own class Amazing Fact Book or some version of it. For example, instead of *Ripley's Believe It or Not*, your book could be "Room Five's Believe It or Not!". Students can take turns taking the book home to share with their families.

Recipe: Weighty Words

Notes from the Chef

This activity is great for building vocabulary. The *Weighty Words* books contain clever stories that help us remember the meanings of words.

Ingredients

Mentor texts: *The Weighty Word Book* and *Weighty Words, Too*, by Paul M. Levitt, Elissa S. Guralnick, and Douglas A. Burger

Appetizer

1. Pick out a word from one of the *Weighty Words* books and give students the spelling so they can write it down. One of my favorites is "ostracize," which means to exclude from a group. *The Weighty Word Book* presents a story about a sparrow who is ostrich-size. He brags so much about being bigger than everyone else that they kick him out. This helps explain that he was left out because he bragged about his "ostrich-size."

2. Have them write down what they think the word means. Share a few student responses. Do not give the real meaning of the word yet.

3. Read the story that goes with the word in the book.

4. Ask students to revise their definition of the word. Ask a student to share how the story helped them understand and remember what the word means.

Cooking Demonstration and Practice

1. Read a few more of the stories in the book to help students get more inspiration. For example, there is a story about how to remember the word "hibernate." It is about a bear named Nate, who is hyper. If you want to sleep through the winter, the story tells us, we should do the opposite of "hyper-Nate."

2. Place students in pairs, unless some prefer to work independently. Either give them a word to create a story around or allow them to choose one. The hardest part of this exercise is figuring out a word that sounds like two other words in some way.

3. You could have someone write about the word "tolerant." It could potentially be a story about a "taller ant." You could have someone write about the word "suitable." Here is a student sample of a story for that word:

"Sam, get ready for the wedding!" said Mom.

"Oh no! I have nothing to wear! I can go to Bobo's Tuxedos," said Sam.

"Hello, welcome to Bobo's," said Bobo. "Can I help you?"

"I need a suit," said Sam.

"Alright," said Bobo. "Here is our cheapest one."

"$1230!?" Sam screamed with rage. "There is not a suit that I am able to afford."

So remember, when you can't find something good enough, think about Sam and his problem. You will remember the word "suitable."

Dessert

Choose a few students to share their word. Ask them to define it, then read their stories. See if their stories help kids to understand the meaning of the words.

Recipe: Picture Prompts

Notes from the Chef

They say a picture is worth a thousand words, right? Maybe you already have a collection of fun picture prompts, but if not, I encourage you to check out these websites. You will find all kinds of interesting photos you can use.

Ingredients

The following websites:

New York Times, What's Going on in This Picture: `https://www.nytimes.com/column/learning-whats-going-on-in-this-picture`

Life Magazine Archives Database: `https://books.google.com/books/about/LIFE.html?id=R1cEAAAAMBAJ`

Popular Mechanics Archive Database: `https://books.google.com/books/about/Popular_Mechanics.html?id=49gDAAAAMBAJ`

Appetizer

1. Show a picture from one of the suggested websites. You will find photos from the interesting to the absurd! Kids will see things in older *Popular Mechanics* magazines that are now antiques they have never heard of! Share many examples and let the kids pick one for you to write about.

Cooking Demonstration and Practice

1. Once your students have picked a photo for you, brainstorm all of your observations about what is going on in the picture. Make a list of what you notice.

2. Tell students they are going to have to pretend they are a writer for the newspaper or magazine that has this photo in it. They are tasked with writing a story to go with the photo. Of course, you don't know the real story, so you have to make it up and it needs to be believable so you don't get fired. Model coming up with a story that explains what is going on in the photo.

3. Allow students to choose an image. They need to brainstorm a list of the things they notice going on. Then they can craft a story for their newspaper or magazine. If possible, allow them to print off the picture to put with their story or copy and paste it into a document to write about.

Dessert

Allow several students to share their magazine/newspaper articles and photos.

Recipe: Squiggle Story

Notes from the Chef

This writing activity is well-suited for younger students. It is taking something that is out of our control–a random mark on the page–and controlling what it becomes. Kids get to be creative in the visual representation of their mark. Then they get to make a story or description to go with it.

Ingredients

Squiggle Template PDF

SQUIGGLE STORY	SQUIGGLE STORY	SQUIGGLE STORY
BY:	BY:	BY:

Thick black marker

Crayons

Appetizer

1. Pass out the Squiggle Story papers to the kids in the room. Tell them they cannot write anything yet. They have to sit and wait to see what you do to their paper.

2. Go around with a thick black marker and put a squiggle mark on each child's page. Each one should be different. You can do a swirl, a shape, or a jagged line. Students will probably react with puzzled looks or giggles.

3. Ask kids what they think their line represents. What could it be turned into?

4. Don't let kids write anything yet.

Cooking Demonstration and Practice

1. Have a student come up and draw a squiggle on your paper with the black marker.

2. Make your squiggle into a picture of some kind. It could be an animal, a roller coaster, a flower, or a funny hat!

3. Color your picture and give it some details.

4. Ask kids what they think is going on in your picture.

5. On the lines below the picture, compose either a short story or a description of your picture.

6. Allow students to create a picture out of their squiggle and color it.

7. Have them write a story or description to go with it.

Dessert

These make a fun display or you can let students take turns showing their squiggle and read what they wrote.

Recipe: Fractured Fairy Tale

Notes from the Chef

I'm sure you've read many fractured fairy tales. I've actually written many of them myself and had so much fun creating silly plot twists. There are all kinds of mentor texts out there to choose from for inspiration. Be sure to get a bunch from your library for kids to read leading up to this lesson.

Ingredients

Several versions of the same fairy tales
Various fairy tale books (There are a dozen "Classic Fairy Tales with a Twist," by Shannon Anderson available from Seahorse Publishing.)
Chart paper

Appetizer

1. Share several versions of the same fairy tale with students throughout the week. Create a chart to compare key elements of the different versions. Add to the chart as you go along. For example, there are many versions of Cinderella. The chart would have the titles or book covers on the left and columns for Country/Culture, Characters, and Symbol.

2. Each day, after reading that version, fill out the chart for that book. By the end of the week, you should be able to see how the stories differ based on the cultures represented, the various differences in the Cinderella character, her family members, and the fairy godmother figure. There is often a different symbol than the glass slipper in the other versions as well.

3. Have students think about a fairy tale they would like to fracture in some way.

Cooking Demonstration and Practice

1. Choose a completely different fairy tale and run through ways you could change an element to give it a new twist. Model rewriting a fairy tale of your choice. For example, maybe you could retell "Goldilocks and the Three Bears" with Goldilocks stopping by the bear's home because she needed to go to the restroom. The bears have left pizza out instead of porridge. Giving it a more modern twist can add some humor.

2. Allow students to choose a fairy tale and twist the plot or story elements to create a different version of the story. If time allows, you could let them illustrate their stories as well.

Dessert

Allow students to share their stories with a partner. You may want to choose one or two to share with the entire class as well. These are a favorite to share with kindergarten and preschool classes too!

Recipe: Tiny Teacher

Notes from the Chef

I did this lesson for the first time during the pandemic. When we were all kicked out of school in March 2020, I decided to mail each student a letter, along with this little cutout of me. I included the directions and explained further in our class Zoom meeting. They each had to come up with a story of how I shrunk and take me on an adventure at their homes or outside. Then they came up with a story about how I got back to normal size. They shared their stories online with our class and they were hilarious.

Ingredients

A color picture of you, sitting or standing, from four to seven inches tall
A color picture of each student, sitting or standing, also four to seven inches tall

Appetizer

> Ahead of time, take pictures of your "Tiny Teacher" picture around your house with pets or outside or in the classroom.

1. Show students pictures of you as a "Tiny Teacher" in different settings. Ask them to come up with possible ways you may have shrunk down to mere inches. Examples could be a magic potion, a shrink-ray gun, eating spoiled food, being crushed by something heavy, a magic spell, or other imaginative methods.

Cooking Demonstration and Practice

1. Model writing a story about how you shrunk, what adventures you went on (based on the pictures you took of yourself), and how you returned to regular size.

2. Pass out the students' pictures. Allow them to cut them out closely, so no background is showing.

3. Allow students to brainstorm ways they shrunk down to this size.

4. Students can brainstorm possible adventures their tiny self can go on when they get home from school and what pictures they need to take.

5. Allow students to take home their tiny versions of themselves to take pictures around their homes or outside, or wherever they want to take them. They need to bring these back to school the next day.

6. When students return the next day, they will continue on from where they left off the day before. They will share the adventures they went on as a tiny person and then come up with the way they returned to normal size.

7. Allow students to compose on devices if available so they can upload their pictures to their stories. Print them off in color, if possible and staple the pages like a book or bind them.

Dessert

Allow a few students to read their story aloud to the class. Allow all students to share their stories with a partner. These are great to share with another class or grade level as well. They could also be stapled up in the hallway for passers-by to enjoy.

Recipe: Branching Narrative Story

Notes from the Chef

A branching narrative is the genre of the Choose Your Own Adventure series books. It is also known as interactive storytelling because readers get to choose what happens next at certain points in the text. These are sometimes tricky to write. The challenge when writing them is the logistics of the page numbering and the complexity of juggling several different plot choices. Using a flow chart can help kids plan. I suggest limiting the number of choices the first time you introduce this genre. For the youngest writers, you may even just start them out by allowing alternative endings as the only choices.

Ingredients

Branching Narrative PDF

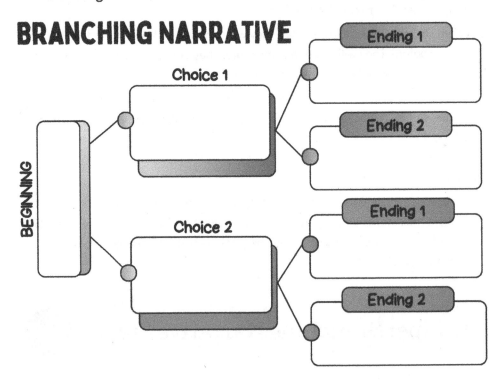

BRANCHING NARRATIVE

Choose Your Own Adventure series books as mentor texts

Appetizer

1. Read one of the *Choose Your Own Adventure* books with your class. At each spot where a choice is offered, let your students vote on what action they want to happen next. (Depending on which book you read, it could take several days to get through the whole thing to the end.)

2. When you finish the book, project up the Branching Narrative chart or draw one on the board or on chart paper. Go to the first set of choices and fill in the two choices that were given (in note form).

3. Go through one choice until it gets to the next branch and fill out the two choices for that one as well.

4. Go back to the other first choice and follow the other choice selections. Fill out the chart for those. This should take you to the end of the PDF chart. (The book will most likely have more choices than that when you keep reading, but the students don't need to do more than that.)

5. Doing this shows the back end of the book and how it had to be structured to get the choices planned out.

Cooking Demonstration and Practice

1. This is a challenging but fun kind of writing. Demonstrate planning out a story on the chart. You don't need to write whole sentences, just notes. Jot down what your beginning will be, the first set of choices, then the choices that will branch out from that.

2. This can take a while to plan out, so you may want to read the book over several days during read-aloud time, take a writing block to do the planner, then take another writing block or two to use the planner and write out the story.

3. After planning and then writing out the story, you can apply the corresponding page numbers for your choices and the pages they lead to. It may help to color-code your pages until you know how many pages you'll have.

Dessert

Once students are done with their stories, allow them to trade with each other and read.

Recipe: Newscast

Notes from the Chef

This activity requires a lot of different roles. Some students will be news anchors, while others are making commercials. Whatever their role, students will be writing scripts for their part of a newscast segment. Be sure to video your end result and let the kids watch it afterward. It's so much fun!

Ingredients

Link to a newscast
Props

Appetizer

Show a snippet of a TV newscast. (Be sure to preview it ahead of time to make sure it is school appropriate.) This could be a snippet of a little bit of news from the news anchors, a weather report, maybe an interview, a sports report, and a commercial.

Cooking Demonstration and Practice

1. Discuss how the TV shows, movies, and even cartoons follow written scripts. The actors and anchors don't just come up with something to say on the spot. They have scripts to follow, which are created by writers. It is another form of writing.

2. Remind students that they learned how to write a reader's theater script back in the "Stick with the Script" writing lesson. The script for the newscast they are about to write will be written in a similar format.

3. Share the different scripts that would need to be written to fill all of the roles for a newscast. You could have two main news anchors, a couple of on-the-scene reporters, a sports reporter, a weather person, people being interviewed, and people to write and act in the commercials.

4. Divide students into pairs and groups to work on the various scripts. Guide students as they are writing.

5. If you have the capability and have a green screen, you can have kids in charge of making backdrops for the newsroom and scenes as well.

Dessert

This is the fun part! Bring in props and have students dress the part for their various roles. You can either just act it out in the classroom or video it to make a newscast that you can share with parents or other classes.

Poetry

Poetry is often not included as one of the writing standards we need to cover in the curriculum. I can tell you that it is one of the best ways for kids to fall in love with writing and to learn how to be creative with their words. Poetry is an entry point for some kids to see themselves as writers. You can sprinkle in poetry throughout the year as a treat for kids to get their creative juices flowing. Or, if you prefer, you could do a special poetry unit and recital in April, which is National Poetry Month. I prefer to use it as a means to practice figurative language and word play. It helps writers to think more intentionally about their word choices. It's an enjoyable process with a fun product at the end.

Recipe: Rhyme Time!

Notes from the Chef

Kids recognize a rhyming poem when they hear you read it. They don't always know that poets use all different kinds of rhyming schemes. I like to project up and read various poems with all kinds of rhyming schemes to see if students can spot the differences. For example, the "Roses Are Red" poem has an ABCB rhyming pattern. Other poems are written in couplets where each two lines rhyme. This would be an AABB rhyming pattern. There are many other types out there.

Ingredients

Various rhyming poems and books written in rhyme.
Where the Sidewalk Ends, by Shel Silverstein
Penelope Perfect, by Shannon Anderson

Appetizer

When you ask students which words at the ends of lines rhyme, they start to notice what patterns emerge.

1. Project up Shel Silverstein's Poem "Sick." Here is an excerpt, with the rhyme scheme labeled:

   "I cannot go to school today," **A**
   Said little Peggy Ann McKay. **A**

"I have the measles and the mumps, **B**
A gash, a rash, and purple bumps. **B**
My mouth is wet, my throat is dry, **C**
I'm going blind in my right eye. **C**

Project up a page from *Penelope Perfect*:

They call me Penelope Perfect. **A**
If you know me, I'm sure you agree. **B**
Have you ever heard of Old Faithful? **C**
Well, that geyser has nothin' on me! **B**

You can project up other poems you find with different rhyming patterns as well.

2. Allow students to go through the poems and rhyming books you have in the room to discover different rhyming schemes.

Cooking Demonstration and Practice:

1. Model writing a couple of poems using different rhyming schemes. You can write something with all lines rhyming, like this:

Saturday is all mine. **A**
Sleeping in 'till past nine. **A**
Please let the sun shine. **A**
A lazy day would be fine. **A**

You can write this one and let students help you finish the last two lines, following the ABCB pattern:

Roses are red, **A**
Violets are blue, **B**
_____, **C**
_____. **B**

2. Let students choose a rhyming scheme to try. They can pick a topic from their ME Page or Expert List, or come up with some other idea. If they finish before the time is up, encourage them to try one or two more different patterns.

Dessert

Have a few students share in class. You could also make a poetry anthology class book out of their poems if you want to let them also illustrate them. This could even be a collaborative project with the art teacher.

Recipe: Haiku

Notes from the Chef

A haiku is a Japanese form of poetry most often used to describe something in nature. For this lesson, I focus more on having kids use the correct number of syllables on each line. If they prefer, they can choose a topic that has nothing to do with nature at all!

Ingredients

Haiku examples
Haiku "recipe"
Chart paper or whiteboard

Appetizer

Ask students what syllables are. Explain that they are parts of words. Many times, we count syllables by clapping out the beats of a word. For example, po-e-try has three syllables. (I encourage students to stick out a finger for each beat rather than clap. This immediately lets them know how many syllables there are without having to clap and count at the same time.)

A haiku is a poem that has a certain number of syllables in each line:

- First line: five syllables
- Second line: seven syllables
- Third line: five syllables

Show students examples of haikus. You can use these or make up your own:

Dolphins
Dolphins are squeaky.
It looks like they are smiling.
Dolphins love to play.

Grasshopper
He jumps in the air.
Landing for just a moment,
Off he goes again.

Cooking Demonstration and Practice

1. On a whiteboard or chart paper, choose a topic to write about. This can be from your ME Page, Expert List, or any random person, animal, place, or object. Explain

that haikus are a Japanese form of poetry typically about nature, but can be about anything you'd like. Write your topic (title) at the top of the paper or board.

2. Allow students to help you think of one thing you want to say about that thing. How could you say it in five syllables? Think aloud and take suggestions. Repeat this for the second and third lines of the poem. Read the finished poem aloud.

3. Ask students to choose something from their ME Page or Expert List, or they can write about another idea. Have them title their poem with this topic idea.

4. Allow students to write their three lines, using the correct number of syllables for each. Walk around to assist as needed.

Dessert

Allow students to share their poems with the class—however many you have time for. If desired, you can do the other poem lessons and have students start a poetry book or journal to record them in. If you want to have a poetry recital at some point of the year, this could be one of the poems your students could share.

Recipe: Cinquain

Notes from the Chef

A cinquain is an unrhymed, five-line poem with a specific number of syllables in each line. Though seemingly simple to write, this poetry form allows you to show the benefit of brainstorming to get just the right creative mix of words. Real writers don't just use the first word they think of. They make lists of possibilities so they have options. Once you have options, you can choose the best combination of words to produce a poem that stands out. This poem also allows you to get a review of the basic parts of speech, too!

Ingredients

Cinquain examples
Cinquain "recipe"
Chart paper or whiteboard

Appetizer

Show students the "recipe" for a cinquain poem:
First line: Noun
Second line: two adjectives describing the noun
Third line: three verbs, ending in -ing

Fourth line: four-word phrase

Fifth line: synonym for the noun

Show students examples of cinquain poems using the ones here, or make up your own.

Dog
Playful, soft
Slobbering, yelping, barking
A friend for life
Canine

Cow
Black, white
Grazing, digesting, resting
A chewing, mooing mammal
Milk-maker

Cooking Demonstration and Practice

1. On a whiteboard or chart paper, choose an animal or person to write about. Allow students to help you come up with two words to describe them, then three -ing verbs, a four-word phrase, and a synonym. Read the finished poem to the class.

2. Allow students to choose an animal or person to write about and put it at the top of their paper. On the back side of the paper, have them make a list of four to six adjectives for that animal or person. Have them look over their list and choose the two most creative or interesting adjectives they came up with. Students can put these into the second line of their poems.

3. Ask students to flip over to the back side of the paper again to make a list of four to six -ing verbs. (These should be actions related to the person or animal.) Tell students to choose the three best or most interesting verbs and put them into the third line of their poems.

4. Tell students that the fourth line is the "heart" of the poem—the line where you come up with the reason you chose that person or animal. What makes them special or cool? What is it about them that interests you? This line can be a short four-word sentence or just a four-word phrase.

5. For the fifth line, they need to come up with a synonym or word that reminds them of the first word. If they are writing about a pet and want to use the name of the pet for the last name, that's fine. This word can be a label. For example, if they are writing about a snake, they could use "reptile." If they are writing about a sibling, the last word could be "brother."

Dessert

Allow students to share their poems with the class—however many you have time for. If desired, you can do the other poem lessons and have students start a poetry book or journal to record them in. If you want to have a poetry recital at some point of the year, this could be one of the poems your students could share.

Recipe: Shape Poems

Notes from the Chef

Any time you can combine creative arts, the process and product are more fun. In this form of poetry, kids will write their poem on the page in a way that visually represents what they are writing about. If they are writing about a butterfly, they could write the words in the shape of the outline of the butterfly's wings. You are using your words poetically and graphically.

Ingredients

Paper
Crayons or markers
Black marker outline templates of animals and objects to use as patterns
Various examples of concrete poems, such as:

Doodle Dandies, by J. Patrick Lewis

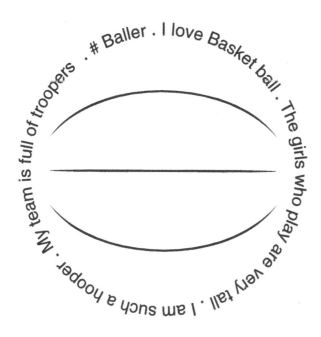

Shape poetry student examples

Appetizer

1. Discuss what shape poems (also known as concrete poems) are. Most poems are written in lines that form stanzas. (Show an example.) Shape poems take the shape of a symbol or object that the poem is about. The words physically create the picture or it. Most concrete poems rhyme.

2. Show several examples of shape poems.

Cooking Demonstration and Practice

1. Demonstrate the creation of a shape poem. Start out by thinking of an animal or object you could write about. On chart paper or your board, write a couplet or two. (This will depend on how big the picture is you are going to make out of your words.) If you chose cat, for example, your couplets may be something like this:

> Buddy is black and white.
> I like to cuddle him at night.
> He really likes his catnip mouse
> And sleeping anywhere in the house.

2. Your next step is to write it in the shape of your poem topic. For younger students, I have some simple black outlines of animals and objects that can be placed behind a piece of paper. You'll be able to see the outline through the paper and

can write the words directly on the lines. When you remove the paper from behind, it looks like you wrote your poem perfectly in the shape of your animal or object!

3. Allow students to look through the templates you have. This may help them decide what they want to write about. (They are welcome to write about something else that they can draw a symbol or outline for.)

4. Have students write one or two couplets about their topic.

5. Give them a blank piece of paper to transfer their words onto in the shape of their object. They can use a template or make their own.

6. If desired, students can color their shape poems for even more visual appeal.

Dessert

Shape poems make an awesome bulletin board display in the room or hallway! Allow several students to show and share theirs before hanging them up. Here are a few student samples.

Recipe: Fingerprint Poem

Notes from the Chef

I've used this poem with elementary kids and even high school kids. Bringing out the watercolor paints is a way to make our words literally more colorful. This poem allows kids to think about who they are and how they are unique. This poem is not rhyming (unless the writer wants to make it that way). Each line starts with a verb to show what the writer hopes for, dreams of, plans to do, and so on. These are beautiful keepsakes.

Ingredients

Watercolor paints, brushes, water
Watercolor paper
Ink pad
Sharpie markers (black medium tip and various colors with fine tips)
Painter's tape
Fingerprint Poem Stems PDF

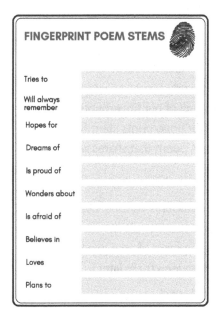

FINGERPRINT POEM STEMS

Tries to

Will always remember

Hopes for

Dreams of

Is proud of

Wonders about

Is afraid of

Believes in

Loves

Plans to

 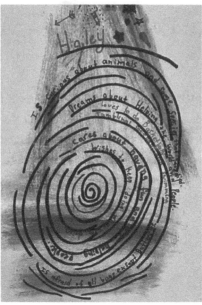 

Appetizer

Pass out a sheet of watercolor paper to each student. Have students press their thumb onto the ink pad and then onto a bottom corner of their paper to make a thumbprint. Allow students to compare their thumbprints to others in the room. Discuss what they notice. Are any the same? What is the same and what is different? Why do police use fingerprints to identify someone? Hopefully, through the discussion, students conclude that all of our fingerprints are different, just like all of us are different as people. Our fingerprints identify who we are. Explain that you will be writing a fingerprint poem that shares who they are.

Cooking Demonstration and Practice

1. Tape up your watercolor page somewhere where students can see. Using your fingerprint on the corner of your page as a guide, use a Sharpie marker to draw a larger version of this on your page. It should take up most of your paper. (Keep the lines far enough apart that you can write words between them later.)

2. Allow students to create their fingerprint on their papers.

3. Gather students back around where they can see. Assemble painter's tape, a cup of water, and watercolor paints. Lay your paper flat on a table. Demonstrate how you tape down the paper on the top and bottom edges. This will prevent the paper from curling up as it dries. Use the watercolor paints to color your entire fingerprint and page. You can do any design or colors you choose.

4. Pass out paints, water cups, brushes, and tape to students. Allow them to paint their pages. Leave them where they are to dry while you demonstrate the next step.

5. While all of your watercolor papers are drying, have students write out their responses to the Fingerprint Poem Stems on the PDF page. Model how you would answer these on your page and then pass out the papers to the students to fill out.

6. Once the watercolor pages are dry, show how you can transfer your sentences of the poem between the whirls and swirls of your fingerprint lines in different colors. Colorful fine-tip Sharpies work well.

7. Allow students to use markers to write their poem lines on their fingerprint pages.

Dessert

Check with students to be sure they didn't share anything too personal. If they are okay with people reading their poems, you can feature them on a hallway or classroom bulletin board display.

Other Writing Forms

There are other valuable writing forms that have slightly different purposes and styles. Here are some ideas for getting your students to write using less traditional methods. The point is to get kids writing and to see how useful it can be, whether to reflect, to take notes, or as a means to complete a project.

Recipe: Daily Journaling

Notes from the Chef

Recording my thoughts in a journal/diary is what got me hooked on writing as a kid. To this day, I keep a journal, even though I only write in it from time to time. Having kids keep a writing journal is a great way to hook some of your students on writing too. It is low-stakes, informal, personal, and not graded.

I used to have my students write in their journals first thing in the morning because they carry a lot of emotions and experiences with them into school. Something exciting *or* devastating may have happened the night before or even that morning. Students know that what they share in this personal journal will only be read by me and not shared with anyone else. It is a special bonding activity for you and your students, in addition to an authentic writing opportunity outside of your writing block.

Ingredients

Student journals
Class journal
Image samples of past class journal pages

Appetizer

Share images of past class journal pages. If this is your first year, you can make up a few on your own. Create a few "pretend" awesome class journal pages written on and commented on by past students. An example could look something like the page shown here.

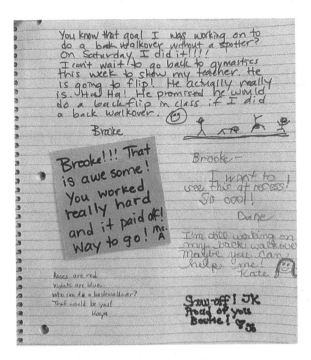

This class journal will be passed around to a different person each day to write in. It is an opportunity to share your own stories, thoughts, or ramblings. You also get to read what others have written before you and comment on their page.

Cooking Demonstration and Practice

1. At the beginning of the year, either have kids bring in a blank journal or notebook or provide one for each student. Explain that each day they will have about 10 minutes to write in their personal journals. They can write anything they want about themselves, their feelings about something, their concerns, goals, or something they want to ask you. Let them know that you will be reading and responding to each person once a week. (However, I always tell students that if there is something that they really need me to respond to that day, they can leave their journal on my desk to read.)

2. Protect this journaling time in the morning. It can be your "bell work" or something they do before or after the morning announcements. It should become a habit for your kids to get their journals out and write something in them.

3. One student each day will receive the class journal. This is a special journal introduced on the first day. When it is a student's turn for the class journal, they can read what others have written and leave comments, congratulations, or reactions. They also get a chance to write something of their own for students to comment on. This is a coveted day when it's your turn to write in the class journal!

Dessert

I used to use a color-coded sticker system for my students' journals. Each color represented a designated day that I would collect it. For example, I would read and respond to red-stickered journals on Mondays, blue stickers on Tuesdays, and so on.

It doesn't take long to flip through and leave little comments or questions when you only have four or five journals a day. I also collect the class journal each day to make comments in.

Students *love* the interaction from you in their journals. Many keep these for many years after they leave my classroom as a keepsake. This is also how I'm able to keep a pulse on my students. They often share things that may be hard to talk about in person. Sometimes kids will share things that are going on with friends in the classroom or at recess. I have also had kids share some very personal things that required help from authorities. I cannot stress enough how valuable this journal writing time can be for your students.

Recipe: Writing from the Wild

Notes from the Chef

When I see one of the books I've written at a bookstore, library, or school, I call it a spotting in the wild. It is a thrill to witness! I call this activity Writing from the Wild because it is an opportunity for students to bring in real writing from their world and share it.

Ingredients

Some of *your* writing samples

Appetizer

1. Ask students what kind of writing they do outside of the classroom. Many may think they don't write at all until you remind them that even sending a text is writing.

2. Show students samples of some of your writing from the "wild." This can include shopping lists, a poem, a letter, an email, a note to or from one of your kids, a lesson idea, a recipe, a to-do list, or even a sign you made, like "Do NOT eat these brownies!"

Cooking Demonstration and Practice

1. Brainstorm on a chart together the kinds of writing we all do outside of the classroom, such as:

   - To-do lists
   - Reminders
   - Diary or journal entries
   - Poems
   - Invitations
   - Jokes
   - Letters
   - Book or movie reviews
   - Notes
   - Signs
   - Recipes
   - Plans
   - How-to's
   - Wish lists
   - Goals
   - Stories
   - Comic books
   - Conversation back and forth in a notebook with a sibling on a trip
   - Something they wrote when they were younger

2. Let students take a picture of or jot these down in their writing notebooks. Ask students to bring in some sample of writing on the first Friday of every month (or whatever day you choose) to share with the class. It doesn't matter how small or large. I have had students work on their own graphic novel throughout the year and show their progress each month. Other students may bring something different every time. (Some may forget or have nothing to share.)

Dessert

On the first Friday of every month (or other designated day), have students share their writing from the "wild." Be sure to share yours too! This exercise reminds students that we are all writers inside and outside the classroom. It often inspires kids to think about doing more writing at home as well.

Recipe: Biography Projects

Notes from the Chef

Kids will probably read many biographies in their lifetime. This project lets them pick one person they would like to write a biography about. Whether they choose to present their information digitally, as a role-play of the person they chose, or a traditional report, there is research and writing involved. Having ownership over who they want to learn more about and what way they will present it adds to the motivation for this project.

Ingredients

Various biography mentor texts
Props for you to present a sample biography

Appetizer

Dress up as someone famous and tell about their life. You can share their timeline from cradle to grave, or just the part of their lives that caused them to be famous or recognized. Be sure to throw in some fun facts!

Cooking Demonstration and Practice

1. Show and/or read various biographies of high-interest people. (These could be picture book biographies or chapter books.) Discuss what biographies are and why people read and write them. You could share that these are accounts of someone's life written by someone else. You can compare this to an autobiography, which is an account of someone's life written by that person.

2. Allow students to choose a person they would like to write a biography about. This is more fun when each person in the class has to choose a different person, especially if you plan to let all of the kids share their finished projects.

3. Decide what information you would like students to cover in their biography project. Suggestions include: What are they known for/famous for? Why did you choose them? What did they have to overcome? What led to their success? Where did they grow up? Tell about their family. Share three fun facts you learned while studying them.

4. Provide books and safe websites students can use to research their designated person.

5. Allow students to present the information they learn in their preferred way. Suggestions include:

- A written biography in book or paper form that they read to the class
- A keynote or PowerPoint presentation with slides
- A speech with posters and props
- A song or poem about their person
- Some other creative way to share the information

Dessert

The presentations may take a lot of time to share. You can set up a schedule to have four or five students present each day during writing time or some other convenient time for you.

When it is a student's designated day to share their biography, encourage them to wear something representing their person and bring in props. This makes it a lot more engaging and fun for the presenter and the audience! Consider inviting parents and caregivers to come to the classroom to watch when it is their student's turn to present.

Recipe: Career Exploration Projects

Notes from the Chef

Having guest experts from the community come in twice a month became an annual part of every school year in my classroom. The kids learn so much in the short amount of time each one is there. I try to have these career exploration projects occur sometime in the second semester after they have had the chance to hear about many different careers. Seeing role models from the community share about their jobs inspires kids to want to learn about different careers.

Ingredients

Books about various careers
Safe websites for students to use to research various careers

Appetizer

Consider having a "guest expert" from the community come in once or twice a month to talk about their careers. This is *such* a valuable opportunity for students to learn about different jobs and the people in their community. You can ask the guest the following four questions each time someone comes in:

1. Why did you choose that job?
2. What is the best part about your job?
3. What is the hardest part about your job?
4. What training or schooling is required to do that job?

Cooking Demonstration and Practice

1. After having several community guest experts come into your classroom, share about *your* job as a teacher or a side job you may have. Answer the four questions that you ask your guests.

2. Allow students to explore a career that they think would be cool to learn about or eventually do. Provide books and safe websites for researching.

3. Require students to answer the same four questions about the job they are exploring in a slightly different way:

   1. Why did you want to explore this career?
   2. What do you think will be the best part about it?
   3. What do you think will be the hardest part of the job?
   4. What training or schooling is required to do this job?

4. Have students choose a way to present their project to the class, such as:

   - A written form that they read to the class
   - A keynote or PowerPoint presentation with slides
   - A speech with posters and props
   - A song or poem about their career
   - Some other creative way to share the information

Dessert

The presentations may take a lot of time to share. You can set up a schedule to have four or five students present each day during writing time or some other convenient time for you.

When it is a student's designated day to share their career, encourage them to wear something representing their job and bring in props. This makes it a lot more engaging and fun for the presenter and the audience! Consider inviting parents and caregivers to come to the classroom to watch when it is their student's turn to present.

Recipe: Class News

Notes from the Chef

When I taught first grade, this activity was part of my morning meeting and calendar activities every day, starting from the very first day of school. I always had the student of the day choose someone to partner with for each day's news. I did this as an interactive writing with help from the kids. The student of the day and their partner would illustrate it while we finished doing the calendar activities.

Ingredients

Class News PDF

Class News!

Appetizer

Ask, "Why do people watch the news or read the newspaper?" Responses will probably be along the lines of "People want to know what's going on." Or "You get updates on what's happening."

Ask students how many of their parents will probably ask how their day went. Guide a discussion: "How many times have you gotten home from school and you can't think of what to tell your parents or you just can't remember? We are going to solve that problem today. We are going to provide your parents with class news!" (This automatically gives them an authentic audience for the news we share each day, which increases motivation.)

For younger students, I write the news with their help. For older students, you could discuss news items to include and let them go off to write it. You don't have to use this template if you'd rather do it digitally or without illustrations.

Cooking Demonstration and Practice

1. With the Class News PDF projected up or on an easel, ask students how you would write the date. I have them spell out all of it, "Today is Thursday, August 8, 2024." (This is something you will do every day to start the news, so kids get practice spelling the days of the week and months of the year.)

2. Next, ask the student of the day to share something they are excited about for the day. You will now use dialogue to write what they said. "Brayden said, 'Today is the first day of school!'"

3. Next, have the student of the day choose another student who has some class news to share. You will write what this student says. "Jessi said, "We get to decorate our lockers today!"

4. Allow the two students to take the news page, illustrate it, and color it.

5. Depending on your grade level, you could have the two students write the news themselves after sharing orally. Or, if they're not ready to do that, you could write it when they share and just give it to them to do the illustrating.

Dessert

At the end of each month, I used to bind together all of the news pages as "September News," or "November News," and so on. I had a checklist to be sure each student had a turn taking home that month's class news to share with their parents. However, you could do this digitally and send home the news daily, weekly, or monthly.

Recipe: Goal Setting

Notes from the Chef

Although this doesn't involve a *lot* of writing, writing down your goals makes them a lot more likely to happen. I used to have a whole giant bulletin board with the ongoing goals of students. You may have heard of the S.M.A.R.T. method of setting goals, to make your goal Specific, Measurable, Achievable, Relevant, and Timebound. I personally have a growth mindset and believe that all of our goals are achievable if we learn, practice, and don't give up. I also think that if there is a goal that you really want to set, that automatically makes it relevant because you care about it.

With this in mind and to keep goal setting as simple as possible for kids, I shortened it to S.E.T. This is explained below in the lesson.

Ingredients

Goal PDF

S.E.T. YOUR GOAL

Specific _____

Effort _____

Time _____

Appetizer

Show students how to set a goal using the S.E.T. method:

- The S stands for Specific. What specifically do you want to be able to accomplish or learn?

- The E stands for Effort. What effort will it take to accomplish or learn it? What kind of learning or practice do you need to do? Do you need to take lessons, watch videos, get a mentor, or something else?
- The T stands for Time. This one is twofold. How much time will you practice or learn each day? What date do you hope to reach your goal by?

Cooking Demonstration and Practice

1. Think of a concrete goal you could set. Model writing that goal using the S.E.T. method and then write out action steps. Try to set a goal that you could accomplish in a month or less. You'll want students to do this as well. This allows you to check progress along the way and coach them on adjustments. (If they set a goal to go to college, you don't have much control over helping them achieve it.)

2. Have students think of something they want to accomplish or learn in a month or less. Maybe it is to do a back walkover in gymnastics. Maybe it is to learn their multiples of seven. Maybe it is to type a certain number of words per minute.

3. Using the S.E.T. method, have them write out their goals using the PDF, a sticky note, or some other page. Encourage them to set at least one academic goal and one personal goal.

Dessert

Once students have set their goals, they can put them somewhere visible. I used a bulletin board with the kids' names on it. Each student had room for at least three sticky note goals at any given time.

Being able to see it keeps it on their mind. It also allows you to check up on the goals of students frequently. I used to check the end dates of goals during self-selected reading time each day and ask kids how they were progressing if the date was approaching. I would help them adjust the effort or time as needed.

Once students meet a goal, they can take that one down, celebrate, and write a new one using the same process.

End-of-Year Publishing Project

This is a very special project I started in the spring of each school year. My students would go through the entire writing process to create characters, a setting, and a plot, and write a story that I had turned into a book. Their main character would be made into a stuffed animal as well. This was my favorite project of the year because it empowered students to see themselves as real writers and creators.

Notes from the Chef

There are all different ways you can "publish" your students. Keep in mind that some cost more than others. Because I used a company that made my students' stories into hardcover books, I had to allow the time for the book kits to come in, and for the finished books to be created and delivered. I also used a company to make the students' main character illustrations into plush figures. These can take at least a month to be created and sent to the school. Be sure to start your writing project in plenty of time for your items to arrive before school is out for the year. The writing of the story itself may take weeks of writing blocks. It will also take many hours to illustrate their book covers and story pages.

Ingredients

- Blank books or book kits
- Company or person to make main characters
- Permanent markers and regular markers

Appetizer

I used to kick off this project by showing book examples and video clips of past years' books and stuffed characters. It builds a *lot* of excitement and motivates kids to want to put in the hard work necessary to produce similar projects. You are welcome to share this YouTube video of one of my past years doing the project: `https://youtu.be/wP3gmeNuhNg?si=RCgQ7T6oTCm5HifM`

Cooking Demonstration and Practice

1. Using the character development lesson, allow students to create a character for their story. This could be a person, animal, monster, alien, or even an inanimate object. Students will need to think about the physical characteristics and draw the character the way they would like it to appear in their book and as a stuffed or plastic figure. I collect these the first day to send off to the company or person who will be working on making these drawings come to life. These can take more than a month to create, so I want to allow plenty of time.

2. Take students through the plot development lesson. Students will plan what it is the character wants to do and why. They will need to devise attempts for their characters to get what they want and ways it will not initially work out for them. Ultimately, they need to have the character achieve a goal or solve a problem and wrap up the story.

3. After planning their story plots, review the narrative beginnings lesson for students to write the beginning of their stories.

4. Each day, you will allow students to work at their own paces to build tension in their stories, create attempts and failures, and further their plot along. Students will progress at different speeds. As they are writing, I am coaching them, making revision and editing suggestions, and encouraging them.

5. Some days, I may stop all of them to see if there is a spot they can replace some "wimpy" verbs with stronger ones. Or I may challenge them to add a simile and an onomatopoeia somewhere. One of my goals for this culminating project is for students to bring together the many skills we have worked on throughout the year.

6. As students finish their writing, I go through a final read-through with them to see if there is anything glaring that needs attention. I do not fix all spelling and punctuation issues, although I may point out some of them. I want this story to be their work.

7. Once the text is in great shape, students can begin illustrating their stories. (I find that markers are bright and easy to work with.) I continue working with the students who are still writing as others are illustrating.

8. Once all students are done writing and illustrating, I send off their story kits to be made into hardcover books. If you are just having students write in blank books or on paper, you can skip this step.

9. Optional other fun add-ons can make this project even more memorable. You can have kids create an author T-shirt to wear to the publication party. I usually get a white dress for the kids to draw their characters on. I wear this dress to the party as well.

10. Once the books and characters are shipped to the school, you can do a reveal day—my favorite day of the year! I gather the students around the author chair, where I have a box containing all of their finished characters. I call them up one at a time to receive their book and to pull out their character. Their reactions are priceless. (I record each one individually and stream the videos together.) The empowerment they feel holding this now-tangible thing that they created out of their imagination is beautiful to witness.

11. Give students plenty of time to read over their books and admire their characters. Let them share them with classmates and bask in the moment.

12. If desired and your students have devices that can record videos, allow students to make a one-minute video (or shorter) as a "trailer" of their book and character. (You can use iMovie trailers if they have access to iPads.) They can do it in the style of a commercial or share their process, or just introduce their book and character and read a short excerpt. Whatever they create, you can stream together as one video to show the parents when they come for the publication party. I also add their reaction videos to this video for parents to witness. (If you decide not to do the video commercials, you could just show the reaction videos.)

13. Allow students to create invitations for their parents and grandparents to come to see their creations. You can ask for or provide refreshments as well.

Dessert

Invite parents to the classroom for your publishing party! You can arrange the desks or tables around the periphery of your room to display the books and main characters. Place your seating in the center of the room for parents to view your book trailers. If you made shirts, have students wear them on the day of your party. Display all of the books and characters and allow parents to walk around to see them. Then have them sit and enjoy watching the videos. It's sure to be an awesome celebration of hard work and creativity.

Notes

There are some extra things I did for this project that you may enjoy doing. I also have some suggested variations if funding is a concern.

Party Attire

I purchased a simple white dress each year. I spread it out on a table with permanent markers for the duration of the project. I allowed students to take turns drawing their main characters onto the dress, and then I wore the dress to our publication party. I also bought plain white kids' T-shirts in bulk so that they could each design an "author" shirt to wear to the celebration. (You may be able to have parents donate money or provide the shirts themselves.)

Party Food

I also provided cookies and drink boxes/pouches for the party. Again, you could ask parents or local stores for donations of cookies and drinks.

Books

For this project, I have used a company called Studentreasures for the hardcover books. When I taught first grade, I used a kit for a class book. This kit was free and I also received one copy of the finished book at no cost. Parents are able to purchase a copy of the class book if they'd like one. Or you could secure grant money to be sure each student gets a copy of the book. For a class book, each student has one lined page and a facing illustration page. I chose topics like future careers and biographies for these.

For older students, I would suggest having each student write and illustrate their own book. These kits have seven lined pages and seven illustration pages. There is also an "About the Author" page. These kits do have a cost for each one, which includes a hardcover book after it's finished. Parents can purchase additional copies if desired. If enough teachers do the project at a school, the kit fee can be reduced or free.

If you don't want to use the book kits, you can definitely just have students write or type on paper and bind the books yourself, or purchase blank books. These are available online or through companies like Bare Books. This decreases not only the costs, but also the wait times for the books to come back in.

Stuffed Main Characters

I have used a company called Budsies for my classroom students. They make custom stuffed animals that look just like the students' drawings. I can tell you that they do an amazing job, but can also be quite expensive (over $100 each). I wrote grants to cover the cost of these.

I have also done this project with homeschool groups and community writing clubs. In these cases, I used a local seamstress to create the stuffed animals out of felt. She did a fantastic job creating her own patterns to make the characters look as much like the kids' drawings as possible. I have also had teachers do this project using creators on Etsy. Another option is to use a high school Maker Space or engineering class. Each student could take on one of your students' drawings to make a rendition of their drawing. This could be with a 3D printer, through sewing it, or some other medium. There are lots of options!

Mentor Text List

5,000 AWESOME FACTS (ABOUT EVERYTHING!), by National Geographic Kids

ALPHIE THE APOSTROPHE, by Moira Rose Donohue

AMAZING SPORTS STORIES FOR KIDS, by Eli Spark

ANOTHER POINT OF VIEW Steck-Vaughn series, by Alvin Granowsky

B IS FOR BELONGING, by Shannon Anderson

BLUEBERRIES FOR SAL, by Robert McCloskey

BRIDGE TO TERIBITHIA, by Katherine Paterson

THE CATERPILLAR AND THE POLLIWOG, by Jack Kent

CHARLOTTE's WEB, by E. B. White

CHOOSE YOUR OWN ADVENTURE series from Bantam Books

COASTING CASEY, by Shannon Anderson

COME ON, RAIN! by Karen Hesse

CRAZY LIKE A FOX, by Loreen Leedy

DIARY OF A FLY, by Doreen Cronin

DIARY OF ANNE FRANK, by Anne Frank

DIARY OF A PUG, by Kyla May

DIARY OF A SPIDER, by Doreen Cronin

DIARY OF A WIMPY KID, by Jeff Kinney

DIARY OF A WORM, by Doreen Cronin

THE DOG WHO BELONGED TO NOONE, by Amy Hist

DON'T LET THE PIGEON DRIVE THE BUS, by Mo Willems

DOODLE DANDIES, by J. Patrick Lewis

DORK DIARIES, by Rachel Renée Russel

THE EMOTION THESAURUS, by Angela Ackerman and Becca Publisi

EPIC ADVENTURES OF HUGGIE AND STICK, by Drew Daywalt

EVERYTHING YOU NEED FOR A TREEHOUSE, by Carter Higgins

FANCY NANCY, by Jane O'Connor

THE FASCINATING SCIENCE BOOK FOR KIDS: 500 AMAZING FACTS!
by Kevin Kurtz

FINDING NEMO, by Victoria Saxon

FRANCINE FRIBBLE, PROOFREADING POLICEWOMAN, by Justin McCory Martin

THE GIVING TREE, by Shel Silverstein

GRAMMAR TALES series from Scholastic

THE GREAT FUZZ FRENZY, by Janet Stevens and Susan Stevens Crummel

I AM PEACE, by Susan Verde

I AM THE STORM, by Jane Yolen and Heidi Stemple

IDIOM TALES (8-book set), by Scholastic

IF YOU GIVE A MOUSE A COOKIE, by Laura Numeroff

I LOVE STRAWBERRIES! by Shannon Anderson

INTERESTING FACTS FOR CURIOUS KIDS, by David W. Leon

LLAMA DESTROYS THE WORLD, by Jonathan Stutzman

ME FIRST, by Helen Lester

MOSTLY MONSTERLY, by Tammi Sauer

MOTHER BRUCE, by Ryan T. Higgins

MUDDY AS A DUCK PUDDLE, by Laurie Lawlor

MY HAIR IS A GARDEN, by Cozbi A. Caberera

MY HEART, by Corinna Luyken

MY MOUTH IS A VOLCANO, by Julia Cook

ODE TO THE COMMODE, by Brian P. Cleary

ORPHAN ISLAND, by Laurel Snyder

OWL MOON, by Jane Yolen

PENELOPE PERFECT, by Shannon Anderson

PIG'S EGG, by Katherine Sully

PRUDENCE, THE PART-TIME COW, by Stephanie Laberis

PUNCTUATION CELEBRATION, by Elsa Knight Bruno

PUNCTUATION TAKES A VACATION, by Robin Pulver

RIPLEY'S BELIEVE IT OR NOT!

SCAREDY SQUIRREL series, by Mélanie Watt

THE SNOW GLOBE FAMILY, by Jane O'Conner

SPLISH SPLASH, by Joan Bransfield Graham

STAND TALL, MOLLY LOU MELON, by Patty Lovell

STUCK, by Oliver Jeffers

SUPERMARKET, by Kathleen Krull

TACKYLOCKS, by Helen Lester

THERE WAS AN OLD LADY WHO SWALLOWED A FLY, by Simms Taback

TOO SHY TO SAY HI, by Shannon Anderson

THE TRUE STORY OF THE THREE LITTLE PIGS, by Jon Scieszka

TWENTY-ODD DUCKS: WHY, EVERY PUNCTUATION MARK COUNTS! by Lynne Truss

THE ULTIMATE BOOK OF RANDOM FUN FACTS, by Bill O'Neil

VERDI, by Jannell Cannon

VOICES IN THE PARK, by Anthony Browne

THE WEIGHTY WORD BOOK, by Paul M. Levitt, Elissa S. Guralnick, and Douglas A. Burger

WEIGHTY WORDS, TOO, by Paul M. Levitt, Elissa S. Guralnick, and Douglas A. Burger

WET CEMENT: A MIX OF CONCRETE POEMS, by Bob Raczka

WHAT DO YOU DO WITH A TAIL LIKE THIS? by Steve Jenkins and Robin Page

WHEN SOPHIE GETS ANGRY – REALLY, REALLY ANGRY. . . by Molly Bang

WHERE THE SIDEWALK ENDS, by Shel Silverstein

A Note to Teachers

Just as we are all readers, you are a writer. Your students are writers. All writing should be valued and treated as communication. Keep the focus on your writers, not the writing itself. Your writers are not good or bad at writing based on their penmanship, spelling ability, or grammar usage.

Acknowledgments

I would like to acknowledge the work of the entire team of dedicated people who helped to make this book possible. From Samuel Ofman, my acquiring editor, to Navin Vijayakumar, my managing editor, Philo Antonie Mahendran for helping me with the production process, to all of the people in between handling the rights, sales, and promotion of WRITING FROM SCRATCH, I'm so grateful!

About the Author

Shannon Anderson is currently a professor, national presenter, children's book author, and certified brain coach. She has taught for 25 years from the elementary level to the college level. She also wore the hats of writing coach, gifted coordinator, and mom. Shannon loves to do author visits, keynote at events, and write books to help teachers and kids. You can learn more about her and her work at www.shannonisteaching .com.

Index